Good Show!

A Practical Guide for Temporary Exhibitions

by
Lothar P. Witteborg
for the
Smithsonian Institution
Traveling Exhibition Service

Washington, DC 1981

Illustrations by
Steven D. Schindler

Editor
Andrea P. Stevens

SITES is a program activity of the Smithsonian
Institution that organizes and circulates
exhibitions on art, history, and science to
institutions in the United States and abroad.

Designed by Dennis Pollard,
Beveridge and Associates, Inc.

Printed by Collins Lithographing & Printing
Company, Inc., Baltimore, Maryland

Composed by Carver Photocomposition, Inc.

Library of Congress Cataloging in Publication Data

Wittenborg, Lothar P.   1927-
    Good show, a practical guide for temporary exhibitions.

    Bibliography: p.163
    Includes index.
    1. Art—Exhibitions, Traveling—Technique.   I. Stevens,
Andrea.   II. Smithsonian Institution.   Traveling Exhibition
Service.   III. Title.
N4396.W57   069.5   80-39543
ISBN 0-86528-007-X

Foreword

For nearly thirty years, the Smithsonian Institution Traveling Exhibition Service (SITES) has organized exhibitions for national and international tour. In offering a wide range of exhibition subjects with equally varied methods of presentation, our goal has been to provide greater public access to the nation's collections. To accomplish this, and in fulfillment of James Smithson's mandate "to increase and diffuse knowledge," SITES has organized and circulated exhibitions from the collections of the Smithsonian as well as from public and private collections in the United States and abroad.

SITES has played a leadership role in the museum field in many important areas. We have designed packing and crating specifications which have set standards for many museums involved in their own traveling exhibition activities. We have developed educational and interpretive materials for children to adults and provide exhibitors with background information for program preparation. In addition, we have undertaken sophisticated evaluation studies and have begun to use computers to assist with registrarial duties.

It is with added pleasure, therefore, that we present this volume on the installation of temporary exhibitions. Undeniably overdue in the museum field, the book was developed to serve many audiences. Museums, galleries, libraries, banks, shopping centers, and corporate office buildings all present changing exhibitions. Whether these exhibitions are from SITES, from another traveling exhibition service, from local sources, or mounted from in-house collections, we offer our best wishes for their successful planning and presentation. It is our hope that this guide will become a reliable reference for many years to come.

Peggy A. Loar
Director, SITES

Acknowledgements

The concept for this publication owes much to Dennis Gould, former director of SITES and now director of the Armand Hammer Foundation. His insight, imagination, knowledge of the subject matter, and deep devotion to the aims and goals of all museums, made this project possible.

For assistance with the work itself, I am greatly indebted to Andrea Stevens, SITES Publications Officer; to Judith Harkison, Renata Rutledge and Constance Bond for their sensitive and skillful editing; to my old colleague Ben Kozak and to Sally Perisho, Ken Kratz, Jim Mahoney and the other reviewers for their comments and criticism (although all mistakes in selection or exposition are mine solely); to Michelle Smith for the preparation of the index; to Steve Schindler for his wonderful and often whimsical illustrations; to Dennis Pollard for his tasteful and restrained design of the publication; to Agnes Larson and Linda Bartlett for their typing of the manuscript; and finally a great indebtedness to Albert E. Parr who guided me, challenged me and taught me during my early years in the museum profession.

Lothar P. Witteborg

Introduction

Temporary exhibitions may be found wherever people congregate. Museums and galleries are logical locations, but so are libraries, banks, shipping centers, churches and synagogues, schools, and building lobbies. This book was written and illustrated as a practical and handy guide for the people behind the scenes of every exhibit installation. While the traveling, or loan exhibition is used as a guide, you may apply the principles and information provided here to your own situation.

The book is cross-indexed for easy reference. We recommend a thorough reading the first time; however, if you only need to know how to install a textile, the index will refer you to each applicable discussion: hanging devices, installation techniques, lighting, security, and so forth. The sources and bibliography chapters provide names and addresses for additional information on special topics.

We designed this book to be used in the workshop and in the classroom, to be carried along to the hardware store and lumberyard, or be kept on the gallery cart. The pages lie flat and may be annotated with your own specifications.

After you have used *Good Show!* for several installations, please send us your comments. Your suggestions will be incorporated in future editions.

Andrea Price Stevens
Publications Officer, SITES

Good Show!

A Practical Guide for Temporary Exhibitions

Chapter 1

Advance Planning

1

Advance Planning

Figure 1

Exhibits are environments in which individuals learn and experience on many levels, both intellectually and emotionally.

■ Understanding the Exhibition Objectives

The success of the exhibition experience depends on many things: its educational objectives, the quality of its objects and graphics, its design and fabrication as well as the knowledge and attitude the viewer brings to it. The first three aspects are the responsibility of the planner, who put it together presumably with thought and purpose. The last, the mindset of the viewer, is the true variable and can be totally unpredictable if ignored. But even here, you, the borrower, have some control. By reviewing the exhibit's content, you and the organizer can determine whether the au-

dience will be specialized or generalized. For example, if the show consists of 19th century Dutch porcelain, it will appeal mainly to those with an interest in either 1) Dutch porcelain, 2) porcelain in general, 3) 19th century Dutch decorative arts, or 4) Dutch cultural history. Attendance here will be limited to a relatively small, distinct group rather than the large numbers attracted to the mysteries surrounding the 18th dynasty of King Tut. If you fully understand the scope of the presentation, then you can effectively plan related activities such as the opening (page 24), public relations and advertising (page 23) and education programs (page 22).

■ Expanding the Exhibition with Your Own Objects

If there is any good reason for doing so, you may wish to add some of your own collection to the exhibition. Including objects from your own collection may enhance the loan material, highlight a local interest or event, expand upon a sub-theme for which your own collection is ideally suited.

Preparing an exhibition is a lot more than simply gathering together several objects and placing them in a pleasing arrangement. When selecting your own things, ask the question: *What* do I wish to accomplish? It may be sharing information, changing attitudes or simply providing an aesthetic experience, or it could be a combination of one or more. Also, what are the special needs and interests of your anticipated audience? If you fail to answer such questions completely, you cannot design valid measuring tools to determine your program's success. Everyone wants to have an effective, successful exhibition. Until those responsible for development, however, become more analytic and more concerned with objectives and evaluation, a poor product will surely be the end result.

When developing an exhibition or when adding your own collections, be sure there is a theme based on solid, scholarly information and that the subject, if didactic, is appropriate for the visual medium.

In preparing an exhibit it is imperative to check your insurance status, getting all the essential data from your lender as well as from your own insurance agent, so you are sure to have the best possible coverage for both objects on loan and those from your own collection.

Consider that the impact of viewing an object of great beauty, antiquity, or scientific importance, however great, only prepares one for further learning. If the interest is kindled and left unsatisfied, the viewer becomes frustrated and passive. You, therefore, have an obligation to supply sufficient information along with the exhibition (not necessarily through lengthy labels) or to list sources for further study. You may wish to prepare a bibliography or essay, charging a small fee to cover your reproduction costs.

■ Adding Audio-Visual Devices

The use of slides or film in an exhibit environment should supplement as well as reinforce the exhibition and further its purposes. To show on film the same objects contained in the exhibit is meaningless. However, to enlarge details or to compare objects with various types and dimensions of design elements; to demonstrate techniques or uses; or to show in what context they were found are all valid ways to utilize audio-

Figure 2   Avoid two to three hundred-word labels to describe the objects. Take another close look at your theme. Something is wrong if it cannot be expressed primarily through objects and pictures. Chances are you are not using the exhibition medium effectively.

visual programs and will benefit the public educationally.

Also, avoid letting the AV dominate the exhibition. The exhibit is what people have come to see. It should be complete without the AV. Should the AV equipment fail as it so often does, the visitor should still have the feeling that the experience has been a complete one. It is good to display a title panel explaining the AV presentation as well as to have available an ''out-of-service'' sign in case of mechanical failures.

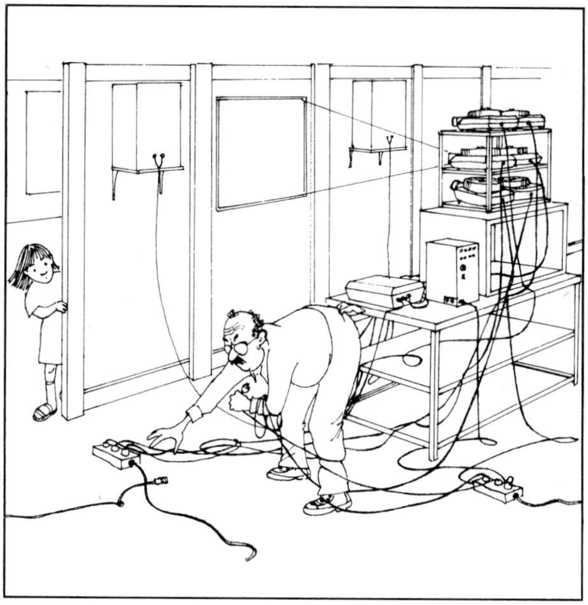

Figure 3 The use of audio-visual techniques can become an end in itself instead of a supplement, involving high costs, extensive, maintenance, faddishness and gadgetry that may distract from the featured objects.

■ Planning Your Own Space

There are various types of traveling exhibitions—some contain only three-dimensional objects; some only two-dimensional ones such as paintings, graphics and watercolors;others consist of graphic panels, dioramas and other special installations.

Sometimes exhibitions come complete with exhibit cases. When you contract for the show of your choice, the organizer will give you a fairly detailed description of the size of the exhibit (in running feet for a wall-hung unit; or square feet for one free-standing), its contents, including the number of objects, and the number and sizes of panels. You will also receive information about the number of crates to be shipped and their weight, as well as specific suggestions for installing the exhibit. In many instances the organizer will furnish, in advance, photographs of the objects, indicating size and color. For more complex units, the organizer may send layouts, plans and photographs showing a previous or completed installation.

This information should be in hand at least two months in advance, so that you, your staff or your volunteers can begin planning. If you have a

special area for temporary shows, you already know how to use it. However, if it is not available or cannot accommodate the show, a new area will have to be cleared and secured.

Lighting should be an important consideration in your choice of space. This space will need to have sufficient light from ceiling fixtures or a ceiling that can accommodate temporary fixtures. If the ceiling is not high enough, lights may be attached to the exhibit structure.

The amount of window light or skylights may be an important consideration since many exhibits contain items that could be faded and damaged by sunlight, by ultraviolet rays as well as heat. Many exhibit organizers explicitly state in their contracts that some of the objects must be protected from both direct and indirect sunlight, since ultraviolet rays bounce. You should be aware of any such restrictions ahead of time and be prepared to block out daylight.

As with most traveling exhibitions, certain rules must be adhered to. The safety of the objects, for instance requires that the space must be secured by guards or an electronic surveillance system. Also, while the exhibition is in your care you must allow only your own professional staff or guest curator to handle the material.

The exhibit should be laid out in such a way so as to permit viewers to move through, around or along the cases and panels with ease. Narrow aisles and constricted areas will block viewing and cause jams, confusion and frustration. Aisles should be wide enough to allow easy exit in case of emergency. Avoid creating a closed passage, or cul-de-sac, where viewers might have a tendency to "pile-up" and then have to retrace their steps along the same passage.

Audio-visual shows should not be viewed across aisles; rather sight lines should be arranged with the screen located suitably for all to see. Their location can be decided on far in advance of the arrival of the exhibit. Remember, also that different projector lenses are available for a great variety of projection distances utilizing a standard-size screen.

☐ *A Scale Plan*

A model of the gallery with cases and panels made to scale from paper, balsa wood and cardboard will help determine the best visual arrangement and visitor flow plan. It is advisable to indicate electrical floor and wall outlets on the model as well as on the floor-plan drawing, in order to provide for case lighting if included in the exhibit. A scale drawing of the ceiling made on tissue or translucent paper (a reflected ceiling plan), showing existing lighting fixtures, is important for placing panels and cases in adequate light. This drawing should be done on the same scale as the floor plan. Lay the ceiling plan directly over the floor plan to accurately coordinate your illumination.

The exhibit may contain only two-dimensional items—paintings or drawings, posters, photographs, or mounted textiles. To arrange group-

Figure 4

A scale model of your gallery made of cardboard or illustration board should indicate accurate ceiling height and placement of doorways, windows and major architectural features.

Figure 5

If panels are to be attached to a wall or hung on picture rods or wire, prepare an elevation drawing in the scale of the walls. Cut out paper panels in scale, corresponding to those in the exhibit and place them on the elevation drawings.

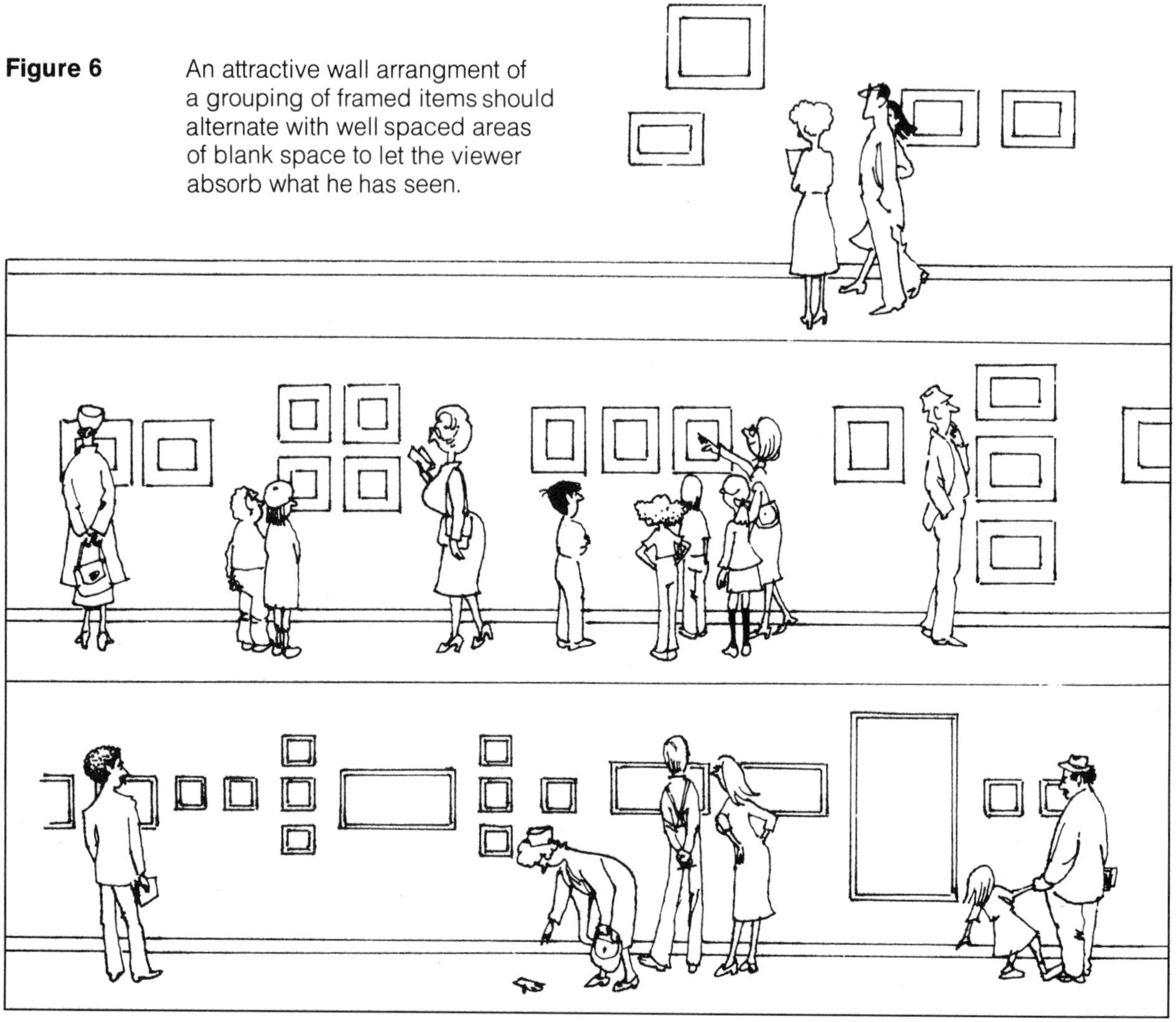

Figure 6   An attractive wall arrangment of a grouping of framed items should alternate with well spaced areas of blank space to let the viewer absorb what he has seen.

ings, make scale cutouts of each article or framed object and place it on a scale elevation drawing of the wall. The lending organization will usually number the framed items in the order in which they suggest they are to be hung. Should you decide to do your own grouping and cluster your framed objects, it must make sense so that objects relate to each other in a logical sequence and carry out the theme of the exhibit.

It is also recommended that you draw a horizontal line, indicating a 5'3" level from the floor, across your scale elevation drawing, as this is the average eye level point used by most museums. However, some exhibits are designed primarily

for children and should, of course, be hung much lower.

If your exhibit includes valuable and fragile three-dimensional objects, you will undoubtedly be required to furnish cases for their protection. Here, too, the organizer will provide a description of each as to size, shape, color and composition and in some instances, a photograph. As before, the first step in arranging this material should be to prepare a scale drawing of each object on graph paper. The scale for this should be larger than that used to plan your gallery space: three inches to the foot is an easy one with which to work.

Figure 7   Each framed picture has an arbitrary "horizon line" within its border: try to follow this horizon line; placing it at an average 5′ 3″ eye level.

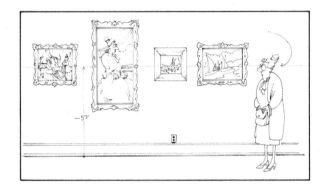

Figure 8   If the frames are the same size, you may use the technique described in Figure 6 by lining them up with equal spacing or you may vary the spaces between pictures for greater interest.

If your exhibit cases are not in use, you might even experiment with a full-scale drawing placed against the interior of the case itself. Backing the graph paper with cardboard will stiffen the mock-up, making it easier to work with. Remember also to plan the placement of labels for individual or groups of objects. Maps, charts and even mounted photographs also lend themselves to display in cases, but be sure they are placed so they can be easily seen and read in the final installation.

If an exhibit of objects comes equipped with its own cases, you will usually receive a detailed drawing of each case showing location and arrangement of pedestals, objects and labels. Objects and display furnishings (e.g. pedestals, risers and holding devices) will all be keyed with identification numbers or letters. Follow the directions carefully and you should have no difficulty assembling and installing the exhibit.

If you wish to add your own objects, you should adhere to the same planning procedures. In order to prevent your items from looking out of place or jarring, select cases, if they are

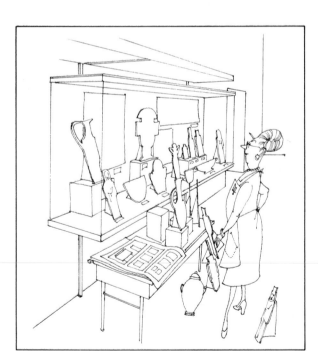

Figure 9   Cardboard boxes used as pedestals with full scale cutouts representing the objects will give you a good idea how to plan an attractive arrangement in the case interior.

Figure 10   Next, prepare a small drawing in plan as well as elevation, noting measurements and identification of each object in the case.

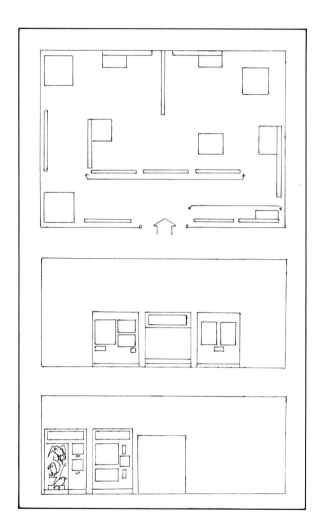

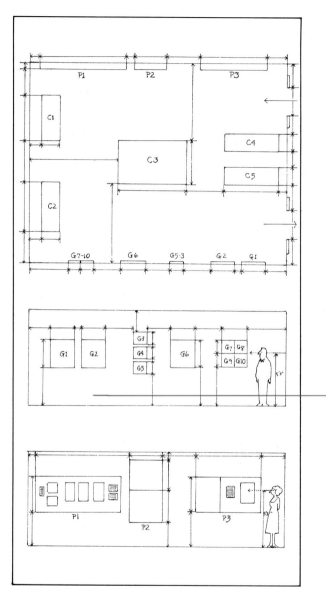

needed, that are simple and neat. Apply the same background color or at least a complementary color, and choose the same typeface for labels and headings for a well coordinated appearance.

Taking the time to do your own floor plans, elevation drawings, reflected ceiling plan for lighting, scale model of the gallery, and scale exhibit cases and objects will enable you to create an impressive and effective exhibit.

Figure 11   When your installation layout is complete, "scale off" two measurements, one horizontal and one vertical, for each element. Also note the numbers of each object, panel or case.

Gallery Check List

Exhibit Essentials	*Your Space*
• Number of running feet of panels	? Total running feet of usable wall
• Number of square feet of structure, panels and cases	? Total square footage of available floor space
• Maximum height of elements	? Ceiling height
• Lighting	? Existing lighting, and if adjustable
• Need to protect objects	? Filters, drapes or blinds to block out sunlight
• Cases for the objects	? Number and size of cases available
• Security	? A security system
• Number of crates containing exhibit	? A secure storage area
• Temperature and humidity	? Climate control

Where to Go for Assistance

Design

Department store window and interior display designers

Theater scenic designers or technicians

Art students

Architects or architectural students

Commercial artists

Fabrication

Carpenters or cabinetmakers

High school/college shop personnel or students

Commercial printers (for label copy)

Lighting

Commercial photographers

Theater-lighting specialists or technicians

Architects or architectural students

Electricians

Department store window and interior display persons

A credit line at the entrance or exit should be given to persons or organizations assisting in the installation.

■ Visitor Flow and Security

Exhibits planners attempt to predict the pace and rhythm of people as they move through an exhibition. Both the planner and the designer want to direct the exhibition viewer's movement so that he sees the display with ease and at his own pace, without getting lost, feeling crowded, or frustrated. But, unfortunately, people never move quite as planned. Therefore you must make allowances for variations in flow and provide for reasonably wide aisles. If a special display, object or audio-visual presentation promises to draw a large crowd, extra space must be allowed so that circulation is not blocked.

An uncontrolled flow of viewers is the more difficult to plan because the layout has to be carefully worked out in relation to both people's

9

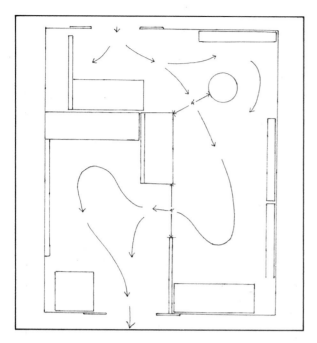

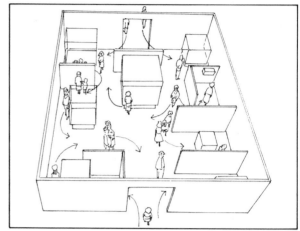

Figure 13 In an uncontrolled flow the visitor may wander around at will which may be preferable for certain types of exhibits.

Figure 12 If you install an exhibit with a flow controlled in one direction to display objects in a meaningful sequence, you should provide a minimum aisle width of at least four feet.

movement and points of view. Furthermore, the character of the exhibit (kind of material, objects or subject matter) and backgrounds (size of panels, cases, color) must also be taken into consideration. As with all studied casual effects, they are usually achieved only through painstaking research and preparation during the planning phase.

Exhibit elements require plenty of space for easy circulation, regardless of whether objects are separated or in groups. Baffles (panels and screens) may be erected to restrict from view areas seen at any one time so the visitor can concentrate on independent groups of logically-related objects as he walks through and around the show. If a free circulation arrangement is appropriate, be sure to allow at least eight feet of space between objects.

Figure 14 Unframed items such as textiles, sculpture, or even paintings may require some kind of barrier.

Figure 15

Freestanding pedestals set alone or in groups may need a rope barrier. They may also be placed behind vertical glass panes held together with Klem fasteners, sitting on 2 x 4s.

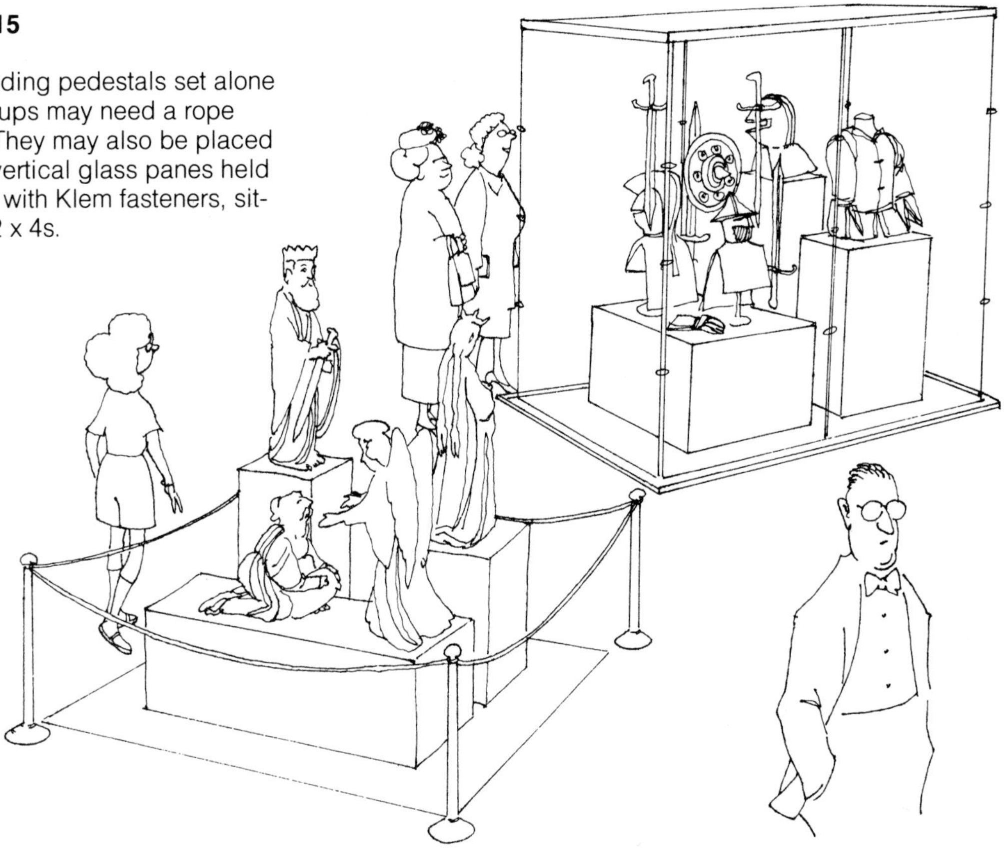

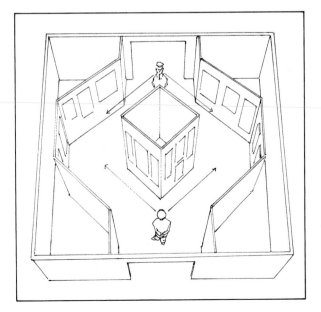

Figure 16   Allow for uninterrupted sight lines in your installation so that a minimum number of guards is required to protect the collection. Avoid creating blind areas that are difficult to observe.

Before finalizing your decisions on sequence, viewing angles and crowd circulation, and gluing the paper cutouts onto the floor plan, there is one important final consideration. This is security. A barrier placed in front of wall-hung objects will decrease your aisle width by three to four feet. Rare, fragile and small items will have to be placed in cases or behind glass. Standing barriers of rope, wood or glass will cut down on your circulation space. All these are factors that will have to be incorporated in your final plans.

11

Figure 17

A striking title panel, an object well lit, an object placed in front of a bold color, or a large graphic image will capture a viewer's attention.

Figure 18

For easy comprehension, design uncluttered wall and case displays, keep labels small and short and use simple maps and charts.

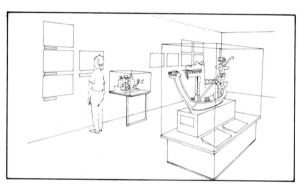

Figure 19 For visual continuity place labels, panels and cases so that the visitor can go easily from one to another.

If a very valuable collection is to be housed in the gallery, security guards may be necessary. Discuss security with your in-house security staff and create an awareness of the significance of the collection to be displayed. If there is no staff, turn to campus or local police. Show them your scale plan and model, and ask for their recommendations for the best possible protection of the exhibit.

■ Design for Communication

Design is the creation of a visual pattern that appeals both to the logic of the mind and to the pleasure of the eye. As the artist-planner sets to work, he or she determines the needs, evaluates the content and develops an intelligent and aesthetic flow of communication to meet the above requirements.

Every sound design solution should satisfy certain basic principles of function, flow, form and communication. What is the exhibit's *func-*

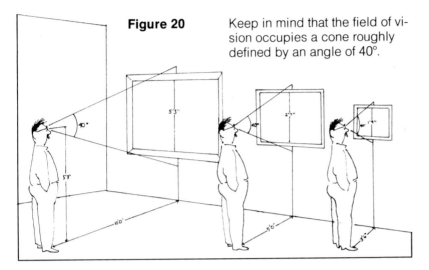

Figure 20   Keep in mind that the field of vision occupies a cone roughly defined by an angle of 40°.

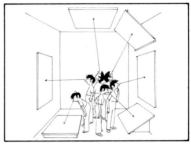

Figure 21

With that in mind objects can be situated so that more than one is seen within the field of vision.

Figure 22   Panels provide additional wall, floor or ceiling planes and perform such functions as support, background and space separation. They have the obvious advantage of being moveable.

tion? How will visitors physically *flow* through or around the exhibit and in what sequence will they view the contents? What *form* will it take—whether with structures, panels, cases, empty space(s), lighting, space and color? Does it *communicate* effectively?

Walls, panels, cases and structural arrangements all serve to place an object within the view of the observer. The most commonly available support surface in most museums and galleries is the wall. You can nail or drill into walls to anchor supports, or you can hang picture wire or rods from a molding and attach a painting, panel, case or object.

□ *Cases*

Cases protect objects and elevate them to a reasonable viewing height. They discourage theft and reduce penetration of dust and insects. Within the case climatic conditions can be controlled, and if required, be altered by inserting hygroscopic (moisture-absorbing) material.

Most cases are constructed of glass with wood or metal as structural elements, or mullions. Some are made of plastic (Lucite, Lexan, Tuffals or Perspex), but a plastic surface needs greater care; with its static-electric properties, plastic attracts dust and requires careful maintenance. For the sake of appearance plastic cases or protective devices must be cleaned daily with non-static

Figure 23

Panels serve as enclosures, support lighting and control circulation. For stability they should be attached at the top or side.

Figure 24

To scale down a large area, change the wall color or add a secondary surface like a painted or cloth-covered panel for a more intimate setting.

cleaning solutions. Plastic also has the unfortunate characteristic of being softer than glass, and therefore scratches more easily.

If cases are used in your exhibit or if glass or plastic is used to cover paintings or graphics, look out for reflections. Glass and plastic must be positioned so they do not shine light into the eyes of the viewer. Reflections and reflected light sources can absolutely destroy a good exhibit.

Bear in mind the following points when installing and placing cases, glass- or plastic-covered graphics:

• Do not place a case or a covered graphic directly opposite a window.

• Do not place a case or a covered graphic facing one another, and especially not two interior illuminated cases.

• Do not place a table case directly under overhead lighting.

• Do not place a table case directly in front of a window.

Some loan exhibits come equipped with cases but because of space and weight considerations no bases are provided. It is, of course, essential for you to know, before deciding upon a particular exhibit, whether if cases are provided, they have bases or supports; and whether they come with their own lighting. You should not contract for

Figure 25

Small objects in a case should be numbered according to the organizer's system. However, if you include your own items, then use your own numbers for greater consistency.

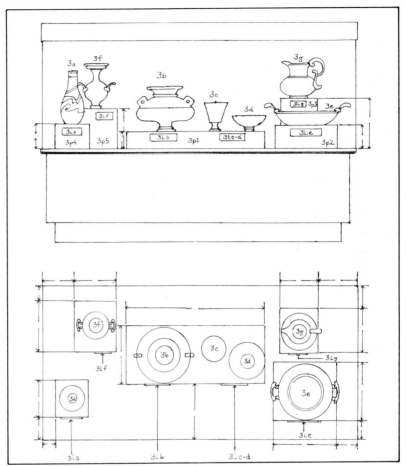

Figure 26

Structures are the mainstay of the exhibit; they can create an intimate environment within the space. They can also highlight an object by setting it apart.

that exhibit if the tasks of providing cases and lighting are beyond your capabilities. But before turning down the exhibit, explore all reasonable sources for assistance, including the ones listed on page 9 .

□ *Structures and Supports*
Structures may be defined as movable exhibit elements which include walls, panels, cases and lighting. They provide stability, pedestals for objects and in some cases, protect against theft. If you use loan exhibits regularly, it would be wise to invest in a commercially-built structural system. Contact several manufacturers regarding a minimal system that will afford you the greatest flexibility at the lowest cost. Be sure to select one

from a well-established firm so that in the years ahead you can still buy parts and continue to add components. When you receive a firm price, look for a sponsor in your community willing to purchase the system. Needless to say, the sponsor should receive prominent acknowledgement. (See page 57 for further description of commercial structural systems and page 160 for names and addresses of exhibit system manufacturers or dealers.)

□ *Color and Light*
Color is a functional as well as aesthetic element in contemporary design. A complex problem, it adheres to no standard rules for its use, but its selection involves such considerations as princi-

ples of aesthetics, physiological perception and psychological effect on the viewer.

Color and lighting play an important role in expressing the mood you want to communicate. Generally, the aim is to create a pleasant environment, neither too dark nor too bright. However, in some instances, a dimly illuminated space may be more suitable for setting the mood you hope to create for the visitor, as long as the objects, graphics and labels are sufficiently lighted for viewing. On the other hand, you may want bright lighting and color for exhibits that deal with such subjects as the solar system, flora and fauna of the desert, Central or South American cultures.

Light should help create the atmosphere of the exhibit, whether it is warm, cool, bright or soft. Some brightness should generally encompass the whole field of view. Shadows should give form and depth to lighted spaces. Glare and distraction need to be eliminated.

If neither an architect nor designer is helping with your installation, ask the exhibit organizers to recommend background colors. For the ultimate environment, apply fresh paint to your gallery! But if the same area is used frequently for loan exhibits, the budget may prohibit a new coat of paint for each show. In that case, select an off-white or neutral shade that will provide a pleasing background for all exhibits.

Some museums and galleries have had success with loosely stretched fabric for a wall covering. It hides nail holes and requires less maintenance than paint. Some have used carpet; however, the expense and the limitation of a "one color" gallery does not allow for much flexibility.

■ Setting Up a Schedule

One of the various difficulties in preparing an exhibition is the time factor. One never seems to have enough time. When you confirm your arrangements with the exhibit organizer you are probably already working against a deadline. When the exhibit arrives, you may have only a few days to install it. This is why all of your planning should be done in advance. As soon as you

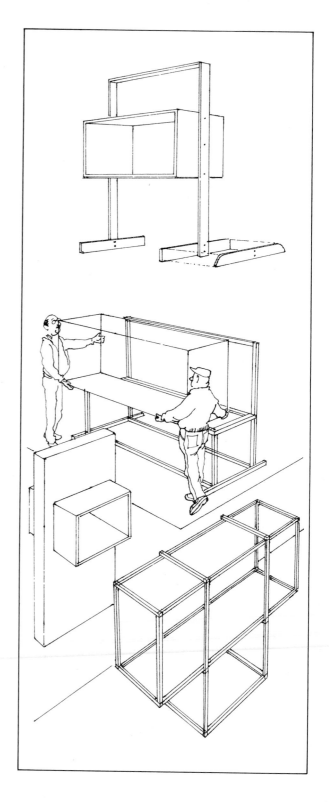

have completed the contractual arrangements with the organizer, you should develop a procedure list and schedule. This enables you to work on a timetable and make sure that you and your staff, volunteers or students do not end up by working a full, uninterrupted 48 hours before the opening or, even worse, right up to the arrival of the first guests on opening day.

The opening day is set. In most cases, the installation period is probably very short. You would do well to prepare a task/time schedule and work backwards from the fixed day of opening. Assume we are discussing an exhibit of ''Early American Agriculture.'' Let us also say that it contains 100 objects (metal, ceramics, textiles, wood or leather) as well as five photographic and text panels and three exhibit cases. It covers about 1,500 square feet (or 135 square meters) and it is packed in five crates weighing some 3,000 pounds.

Because this is a medium-large show the organizers have scheduled a period of three weeks to dismantle, ship and reinstall between closing and opening dates. The period breaks down as follows: one week to dismantle at the previous location, one week to ship and one week for you to unpack and install.

If yours is a small organization you know that you will have to carry the main load. This involves many chores, such as: contracting for the exhibit, writing the press release, arranging for the caterer, ordering flowers and printing of invitations, preparing the installation layouts and clearing and painting the gallery and, finally, handling the objects themselves. However, you will need help with moving heavy units and shipping crates. You may also need help unpacking,

Figure 27

Gallery items other than walls, panels or cases are considered structures. They provide stability, raise objects to a desirable height and protect against theft.

filling out the condition report and seeing to all the final details.

In the planning process, the registrar is the one person usually responsible for keeping track of the objects and for noting the object numbers on the drawings. If there is no registrar, this becomes the responsibility of the curator or director. Someone should also see to such necessities as a comfortable rest area for visitors, access for handicapped, signs announcing publications, tours and lectures, and the location of potted plants or other appropriate decorations at the entrance.

Plants may be used also within the gallery to enhance the exhibit. They may subtly help to direct traffic or emphasize a change in the subject. But plan your greenery in advance; don't bring it in as an afterthought. Have extra ones ready to replace those that begin to droop. Plant maintenance is just as important as clean floors and glass.

We recommend that you sit down with your helpers, whether staff or volunteers, and familiarize them with the exhibit in detail. Give them specific assignments with completion dates. The Task/Procedure Schedule will assist you also in deciding what tools, materials and equipment are required for each undertaking and will enable you to order them in advance, saving you from having to scurry around at the last minute in search of a vital piece of equipment.

The schedule shown on page 18 is only a suggestion. You may develop your own by adding tasks or by eliminating some that are not pertinent. The same procedure should be followed for a small show as for a large show.

Experience gained from other institutions' successes and failures can help you with your own exhibits. It is a good idea to attend other temporary, traveling shows. Speak to the director and inquire about the problems and solutions.

With careful planning and scheduling you will find that the experience need not be traumatic. By soliciting help well in advance—from the community, school or your own institution—you should be able to gather a pool of talent to assist you in carrying out the necessary tasks.

**Sample Task Procedure Schedule
(tasks will vary depending upon
the facility and type of exhibit)**

Task Procedure	Person or Persons	Materials Required
1. Contracting for the exhibit & getting detailed information from organizer, including insurance status. Check also with your own insurance company regarding loan exhibits.	Director or project coordinator	
Planning supplementary and/or educational programs	Education person	
2. Announcement of exhibit to press members	P.R. Person	Press releases, envelopes, stamps
3. Preparation of preliminary installation plans	Designer	Architect's scale, graph paper, drafting tools, cardboard, X-acto knife, tape, glue
4. Consultation with organizer & outside consultants	Architect, designer, security specialist	
5. Preparation of final installation plans	Designer	Final plan & elevation drawings & scale model
6. Discussion of installation	Staff, volunteers, students & maintenance staff	
7. Preparation of poster & invitation designs	Designer & printer	Design materials, as needed
8. Completion of time schedule for exhibit installation & for publicity	Director or project coordinator	
9. Arrangement of catering, car park, cleaning, photographer & other services, e.g., plants for gallery	P.R. Person	
10. Finalizing individual exhibit case layout	Designer	Drafting tools, as #3
11. Mailing press & opening day invitations—putting up posters	P.R. Person	Letters, printed invitations, envelopes, stamps

12.	Clearing a secure space for the shipping crates and their contents for unpacking	Maintenance staff	
13.	Clearing gallery of previous exhibit	Registrar or maintenance staff	
14.	Preparing gallery for new exhibit, i.e., lighting and painting and cleaning of gallery	Maintenance staff, painters & electricians	Ladders, paint, brushes, drop cloth, lighting fixtures
15.	Delivery of exhibit	Maintenance staff	
16.	Unpacking & checking contents & preparing condition report	Registrar	A secure area, work table, dollies
17.	Installation of major elements	Maintenance staff	Dollies, hand tools, extension cord, work light
18.	Installation of all remaining elements	Registrar, project coordinator or designer	
19.	Photographing of objects & installation	Photographer	Camera, film, tripod, lights, extension cord
20.	Preparation of information & photographs for the press	P.R. Person	Press release, photographs
21.	Final lighting	Designer & electrician or maintenance staff	Ladder
22.	Final cleaning of gallery & case interiors	Maintenance staff & registrar	Brooms, mops, sable brush
23.	Cleaning of glass & closing of cases	Maintenance staff	Glass cleaner, clean cloth, sable brush
24.	Placement of plants in gallery	Staff or designer	Plants
25.	Press preview	P.R. Person	Press kits
26.	Private opening ceremony	Caterer, guest speaker, board members, invited guests	Tables, chairs, decorations
27.	Public opening		
28.	Review of exhibit	By press, visitors	A questionnaire (?)
29.	Review planning process & execution of installation	With entire staff	
30.	Dismantle exhibit—add to condition report	Staff & maintenance staff	Dollies, hand tools, work table

Chapter 2

Preparation

2

Preparation

■ Interpretive and Educational Programs

Expanding an exhibition's theme through innovative interpretive programming is a challenge and the resulting effect is almost always worth the effort and cost. Although the organizer of a temporary exhibition may provide you with some materials and program suggestions, you will have to adapt them for your own special use. The exhibition theme, your audience and community, budget, and staff will all be factors in the design of the program you present. Printed and audio-visual materials, performances, workshops, lectures, and special tours are among the programs which will help bring the exhibition to life. Consider the following points:

1. It is essential to involve your entire staff. Communication and cooperation at the beginning among preparators, security officers, curators, educators, and administrators will result in an organized, efficient and well-run program. When planning an exhibition installation, you should

Figure 28

An exhibition may be supplemented with educational programs such as a lecture or film. The organizer may sometimes provide a study guide for use in discussions with younger audiences; it may also supply a catalog and bibliography.

consider your educational program. For example, tour groups will require adequate space for viewing objects or panels; space for holding workshops should be cleared and ideally be located in an area adjacent to the exhibition.

2. If materials have been provided with the exhibition, consider the variety of ways in which they may be used or adapted. For example, catalogs, label copy, or slide programs can be used by tour leaders or docents.

3. Consider your audience. Special interest groups, children, the aged, disabled, young

adults, students, and teachers will require programs for which the format and content is often different.

4. Consider the form the interpretive materials should take. An exhibition may include one or more of the following: publications such as brochures, children's books, handouts, catalogs, or posters; audio-visuals such as slide/cassette programs, films, filmstrips, or videotapes; live performances including concerts, plays, puppet shows, mime, and workshops; scholarly programs such as lectures, guided tours, seminars, and discussion panels.

5. If money for these programs is not available within your institution, you will have to raise funds through other sources. Local resources may become sponsors of the exhibition and provide program support: corporations, clubs or business groups, small businesses are examples. Locate a company or group whose work relates to the exhibition topic. It is in the best interest of most companies to support the arts and humanities. A company's credibility as well as visibility will be enhanced through cooperative programming which gives appropriate credit for efforts and interests. In addition, distributors and educational organizations will frequently donate books, films, and other existing educational materials. Ask them for their order forms with descriptive information.

6. If personnel shortage is a problem, look to your community's commercial or educational institutions for volunteers. A newspaper employee may speak on the development of newspaper printing for an exhibition on the history of news reporting. Equipment may be brought in for demonstrations or else tours of the printing plant may provide an outreach activity. Other souces for volunteers might include local libraries, universities, schools, colleges, historical societies, performing arts organizations, or other museums. Teachers who are planning a gallery field trip will need information about the exhibition far in advance. They can, in turn, provide you with curriculum guidance for your gallery.

7. One should never overlook any suitable resource. Ideas, people, creativity, and money can all work separately and together to your advantage in planning a strong and challenging interpretive program.

There is always more than one method for interpreting an exhibition. The challenge is in finding the most appropriate and effective one for bringing out the best in the audience as well as in the exhibition.

■ Public Relations

In order to attract an audience, "getting the word out" and "the message across" is of vital importance to those involved with cultural institutions. As the range and volume of leisure activities increase, so too does the necessity of bringing information about your future exhibits to the attention of the public. A promotion strategy must be vital and imaginative, and based on good relationships with news media.

Figure 29   Most exhibit organizers will furnish a press kit containing a news release and 8x10 black and white photographs of important pieces.

As soon as the opening date is set, prepare an announcement for the media "calendar" of cultural events. About two weeks before the event, send out a reminder if you want good press coverage. Look for a special "angle" concerning the exhibit that may make a good feature story. Include all the facts in one release, along with the name and daytime telephone number of a contact.

For your media opening, the press kit should include a cover release containing details of the exhibit, perhaps several short releases dealing with items or persons associated with the exhibit, biographies of special guests or lecturer present, and 8x10 black and white glossy photographs with captions. Give credit to the organizer and any source of financial aid that made the exhibit possible.

Not every exhibit will attract the same number of visitors. For those with narrow appeal, there are many things you can do to create wider interest—such as presenting lectures, films and "gallery talks." For the latter, schedule a talk at the exhibit, where visitors can have an open discussion with the speaker. To generate attendance at these gallery talks, however, you must inform the media in advance and follow up with a reminder of time and place.

Here are some tips for audience-building:

- **Press**—Suggest feature articles, letters to the editor, exclusive stories; include foreign language newspapers, company and organizational newsletters.

- **Publicity**—Develop a general mailing list and then break it down into special interest groups. Send brochures, posters and announcements to libraries, schools, banks, colleges, hospitals, clubs, and organizations. Be sure your announcement is included in the "package" mailing of other arts groups. Ask the local Chamber of Commerce to publicize the area's cultural resources.

Figure 30   An exhibit opening should be an event—a time for good will and conviviality. It will make new friends for your organization and result in greater support and recognition.

- **Advertising**—Put across your message on banners, billboards, matchbooks, posters, stickers, school and office bulletin boards, shopping centers, menus, handbills, window displays, bus cards, spot TV ads.

- **Special events**—Sponsor a series of exhibit related events such as a poster contest for high school or college art classes. Present a special evening for the local professional women's organization. Sponsor research studies, and awards and presentations.

■ Arrival of the Crates

When the crates arrive at the loading dock, they are placed on dollies and moved into the unpacking area. They will be lettered or numbered to correspond with to the contents list (manifest). Instructions for unpacking are usually sent in advance by the organizer. Some crates may need to be opened before others since they may contain cases or structural elements that will have to be assembled first.

Needless to say, extreme care should be taken in the handling of the objects. The fewer persons involved in unpacking and examining, the less chance there is of breakage. It is a good idea to make notes of the wrapping and placement of objects, noticing any peculiarity in the position of one object to another. A condition report concerning damage or loss sustained while in transit or at the previous location will need to be filled out. Any problem should be reported to the organizer immediately; he may be able to send you a replacement. He will also need detailed information for insurance claims.

Be sure to store the display items away from the exhibit area until all maintenance staff, carpenters, painters or electricians have finished their work and removed their tools. Just prior to installation, bring in the objects and place them on padded tables. Never leave anything sitting on the floor—you are inviting catastrophe. In addition, never place equipment on the same table with the objects. A careless or quick move can topple a valuable item onto the floor to be forever lost.

Figure 31   While unpacking the exhibit notice how certain objects have been wrapped and placed. Keep all the original packing material to use when repacking.

■ Exhibition Maintenance

Good housekeeping is mandatory if you wish to retain your reputation as a cultural showcase. There is nothing quite so bad as walking into an exhibition and not being able to see it because of dirty glass or burned-out light bulbs. Instill in the minds of all personnel that your gallery is a source of pride. Its appearance should be in mint condition at all times.

Someone should make a tour of the exhibit area at least twice a day to check for dirty glass, refuse on the floor, burned-out light bulbs or graffiti. Conditions such as these invite a poor attitude on the part of the public and may cause serious damage for which you will be held liable.

If case interiors have collected dust, open the cases before public hours and clean the flat horizontal surfaces. Use a soft animal-hair brush so as not to cause any damage to the objects. In

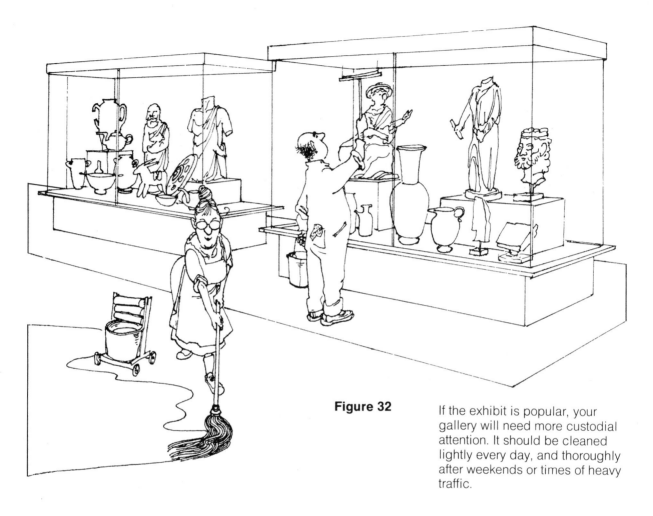

Figure 32   If the exhibit is popular, your gallery will need more custodial attention. It should be cleaned lightly every day, and thoroughly after weekends or times of heavy traffic.

some urban and industrial areas you may note that glass objects and metal (especially silver, brass, and copper) will begin to look cloudy, or even tarnish. If this occurs ask the exhibit's organizer at once for recommendations regarding cleaning. Occasionally when lending an object for circulation in a traveling exhibition, the original lender of the object has placed stringent restrictions on how and by whom that object is to be cleaned. It may be necessary to call in a professional museum conservator to do the work. Therefore, it is best to check with the organizer of the exhibit before some irreparable damage may be unintentionally caused by a well-meaning person.

By the same token, wooden or painted objects

(especially folk art where colors may not be stable), textiles, fur or feathers, and some stone and ceramic items should only be dusted. Never apply water, soap, detergents and most cleaning solvents on any object unless you have specific instructions from the exhibit organizer.

■ Dismantling and Packing

It is easy to assume a lax attitude toward an exhibit that you have been looking at every day for at least four weeks. You may even be anxious to get it out of your gallery and packed because a new and much more exciting exhibit is arriving in a day or two. Do not fall into this trap. Every object shown in your gallery, regardless of your personal preferences, deserves the best possible care you can give it. Carelessness, negligence, or a disdainful attitude will ultimately result in your not being able to borrow or even rent another traveling exhibit. Furthermore, it may lead to your possible liability for loss or damage. The museum gallery community is relatively small; an organization possessing a lackadaisical reputation will soon be excluded from it. On the other hand, an organization that takes particular care of objects in its charge will soon gain a reputation for being reliable and conscientious.

Remember, you are usually responsible for the outgoing shipping arrangements and freight charges. To assure the exhibit's arrival on time at its next destination, make pickup arrangements with your local freight agency or hauler in advance and have all shipping documents filled out *clearly*. Failure to follow shipping instructions, or sending the exhibit to the wrong institution (unless the organizer himself is making the arrangements) will result in you having to pay the rental fee of the next exhibitor, as well as extra shipping charges.□

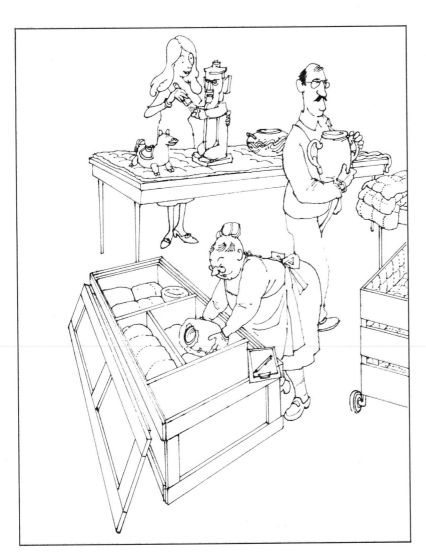

Figure 33

To prepare the articles for re-packing, place them again on padded work tables. Wearing white cotton gloves, the staff should dust each object before it is wrapped. Dirt can be abrasive.

Chapter 3

Fabrication

3

Fabrication

■ **Panel Construction**

Now you are ready to undertake simple tasks of building your own panels and exhibit cases. This guide will not cover every aspect of woodworking, as other publications provide more details. We will only present the elementary principles that require a few basic skills with which you can accomplish satisfying results.

Whether you are adding a few elements to a traveling exhibition or creating one from scratch, you should know the exact number and measurements of panels, pedestals, cases, and other exhibit furniture necessary. If you need help, take the model, scale drawings and fabrication schedule to a lumberyard. Ask for advice: the personnel there are probably accustomed to helping home owners with the "do-it-yourself" syndrome. After all, they will be taking your good money and undoubtedly would like to keep you as a steady customer.

In the design and planning stage for your exhibition, you will decide how many panels you need and how each is to be used. Standardize the panel and case sizes, if possible, so that they will become a permanent inventory. Some light panels can serve as freestanding space dividers or as surfaces on which to mount photo murals or a general descriptive text. Others may need to be

structurally sound to support heavy objects or cases. Additional considerations include whether panels are to be used to cover windows, which ones are to be seen from only one side, and which from two—requiring a finish on both sides. All of these factors will determine how you will build a particular panel.

Our advice is to use good materials, if possible, although it may mean greater expense. The product will last much longer and give more flexibility for reuse. However, don't overlook an old piece of plywood that can be restored with a nice coat of paint. Since most sheet material (plywood, Upsom board, chip board, and hardboard) comes in standard 4'x8' sizes with thicknesses varying according to final use, most exhibits use the 4'x8' size as a standard module for the support panel. Of course there can be variations from narrower to wider panels depending upon space limitations, just as the vertical dimension can be increased in case of high ceilings.

□ *Assembly*

For a simple 4x8' panel of ⅜" plywood framed with 1x4" pine, cut two pieces of 1x4 (actually ¾x 3⅝") pine eight feet long, and two pieces 3'10½" long. Figure 34 explains the frame construction. When it is finished, spread a light coat of glue on the ¾" face of the frame. Place the plywood panel on the frame and line it up along the longest leg. With a 1½" finishing nail, attach the plywood to the frame at about 4" intervals. Then line up a short side and continue nailing until all four sides are fastened. Since the plywood panel is always "square," push the frame (it has enough give) to line up with the plywood before nailing. Drive the finishing nails down slightly below the surface with a nail set and fill the holes with wood putty, using a spatula or putty knife. Sand the putty after it dries. A double-sided panel is shown in Figure 35.

To cover a 4x8' panel with cloth, wrap one face and staple on the reverse side (see Figure 36). Start to staple in the middle of one long side and drive in about three staples an inch or two apart. Then move to the center on the other side of the panel. Pull the cloth as tightly as you can and

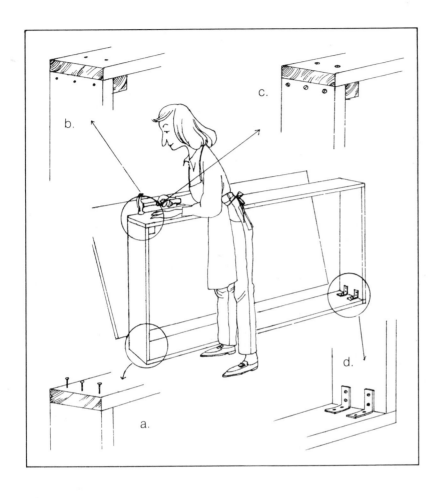

Figure 34 Frame Construction

To assemble a panel, you have the choice of nailing the frame together, screwing it together, or using inside corner braces plus glue. There are also two nailing methods. In nailing method "a" drive the nails through one piece of flat lumber into the end grain of the second piece; in method "b," cut a "glue block" and nail through both pieces of flat lumber into the glue blocks (spread a little white glue on both surfaces of the block). The latter method gives a stronger corner; using screws "c" in conjunction with the glue block makes the corner even stronger. If nail or screw heads are not to be seen, the best choice is the inside corner brace "d."

staple two or three times. (Two pairs of hands can do this better than one.) After the two sides are fastened in the center, move to the third and fourth sides. Complete the stapling, always pulling the cloth taut. If the cloth has a grain or pattern, be careful not to distort the grain. Fold the corners neatly, or if the cloth is too thick, trim the excess just before stapling.

A graceful and dramatic effect can be achieved with a curved panel (Figure 38); however, its use should serve a particular design purpose. Make sure the curve is not just a gimmick. Photomurals, especially panoramic views, are often quite effective when mounted on a curved surface. You can create a horizontal or vertical shape, whichever you prefer. The basic structural principles are the same.

□ *Finishing*

The type of finish you apply to your panels will depend upon the color scheme of the exhibition. The panels may have a natural wood finish, be painted, or covered with cloth.

If you use paint, first prepare the wood surface by sanding and filling nail holes, splits, and blemishes with wood putty. When the putty dries, give it a final sanding. Wipe the entire surface with a clean piece of cheesecloth. Run your hand over it to make sure there are no rough areas. Then prepare the sheeting material for painting.

Since plywood, hardboard, and other sheeting generally have an excellent finish, sand only the sharp edges and spots where you have filled the nail holes. Apply a sealer or primer with a roller or brush; let this dry thoroughly and then apply

Figure 35   Double-Sided Panel

If a panel is double-faced, repeat the nailing process described in the text with the second sheet of plywood; however, you should have two cross braces running across the narrow width of the panel. Use inside corner braces screwed into place.

Figure 36   Cloth-Covered Panel

To attach a cloth-covered plywood sheet to a 1x4″ frame use inside corner braces at approximately six to eight-inch intervals. It is best to screw the corner braces onto the frame first.

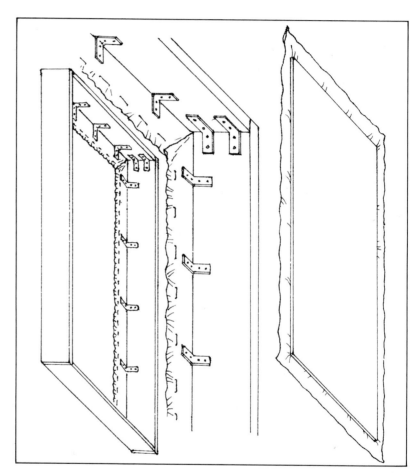

the coat of paint. You can see after your first application if the panel will require a second coat. Remember to place newspapers or a drop cloth on the floor and raise the panel slightly so it does not rest on the floor or lean against a wall.

If you prefer the natural pine finish for the 1x4″ frame and the front plywood panel, sand it carefully. Fill nail holes and cracks with a wood dough applied with a putty knife. When the wood dough has dried thoroughly, sand the filled area smooth with a fine grit paper. You may either stain the wood to match existing elements, leave it natural and apply a clear varnish, or rub it with linseed oil and then paste wax. Staining and natural wood finishing take more time than painting. Always test the finish first on a piece of scrap lumber and follow the manufacturer's directions. If you have any questions, consult a paint dealer or hardware store.

A number of fabrics as well as vinyl, metallic

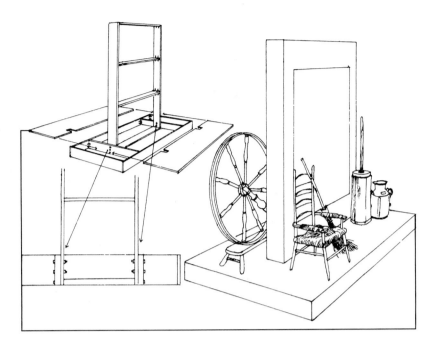

Figure 37   Panel and Platform

You may want to create a
freestanding panel with
surrounding platform on which to
display larger objects such as
furniture or sculpture. Here the
base would act as the prime
support for the vertical panel.
You can vary the size and height
of the base, as well as the height
and width of the panel. This unit
is heavy and difficult to store; we
therefore recommend that it be
screwed and bolted together to
allow for dismantling.

foil, cork, and even wood are backed with paper
or cloth. Some of these wall coverings contain
adhesive and are relatively easy to mount. Most
come in 27″ width, with those of better quality in
54″ width. In some instances you might want to
consider ordinary wallpaper to cover a panel,
such as reproductions of traditional, historic patterns to set off historic objects.

   Some vinyls require a special, strong adhesive,
though most can be mounted with ordinary

Figure 38

Curved Panel

To make a curved panel, cut a
frame out of lumber (if it is
straight and not warped) or
plywood. Brace the frame with
1x4″ pieces glued and nailed on
a ⅛″ sheet of Upsom board (also
called Easy-Curve) or a sheet of
⅛″ bending plywood. Upsom
board comes in standard 4x8′
sheets with special orders, if
quantity is sufficient, up to 4x12′.

wallpaper paste. If and when you decide on this kind of panel cover, be sure you understand what kind of adhesive to use and how to properly hang the covering. There is a ''pre-mixed'' wallpaper adhesive on the market that can be applied directly to the wall, while the covering remains dry. There is also a ''strippable'' paper with adhesive and a backing. Both cost a little more, but are easy to apply.

If you choose traditional wallpaper or other covering, you will need additional tools to do a proper job. ''Papering'' a flat horizontal panel is easier than a vertical wall. Rest the panel on two sawhorses or a large work table. For the pasting, make a table out of a 4x8′ sheet of plywood and two sawhorses. You will need a paste brush, smoothing brush, seam roller, and trimming knife (a sharp mat knife or a single-edged razor blade will do). Pre-pasted wall coverings must be soaked in a water tray, which can often be rented from your dealer at a nominal cost.

□ *Connecting Devices*
In the exhibition environment, panels are used either freestanding, placed against a wall, or hung on a wall. There are rare instances when a panel might be suspended from a ceiling. Figures 41 and 42 explain how to join freestanding panels.

Before installing the units mark their exact locations on the floor with chalk or masking tape. Move the first panel into place (you will need a number of strong bodies for this). Add the second panel and fasten the connecting device. To hold the panels stationary, cut a 3″ length of 3M double-faced foam tape and place it on the bottom edge of each. This fixes their position even during heavy traffic of the exhibition. If the floor is carpeted, secure the panels by driving finishing nails through the base at an angle and into the carpet.

If the floor is uneven and the connectors do not seem to line up, you might have to force a thin tapered piece of wood (shim) under the bottom of

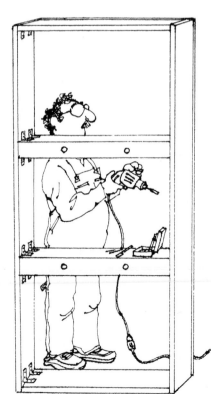

Figure 39   Cross Bracing

Additional cross bracing will be required for a panel strong enough to support a heavy object or a case attached to the front. If you have 1x4″ lumber for the outside frame, use 2x4″ or even 1x4″ bracing for sufficient strength. To assist you with the engineering of the support, consult your friendly lumberyard. Have your weights, measurements and other details ready, such as the weight of the object, type and size of case, contents, and number of glass or plastic faces.

Figure 40   Lightweight Panel

For smaller, thinner panels, make your frame either horizontal or vertical with 1x3″ lumber. If the back of the panel is not visible, use 3″ corner braces and 3″ ''T'' braces for the center crosspiece.

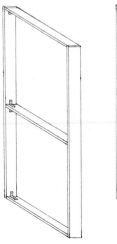

the panel to make it level. Trim off the excess with a sharp knife.

A zigzag pattern can be used for panels set against a wall, as well as with the freestanding units. Here it will not be necessary to cover the back of the panels with plywood or other sheet material. The connectors may also be the same—corner braces (angle irons), butt hinges, or wooden blocks. Figures 42, 43, and 44 show methods of joining panels at the rear.

The two end panels can be secured to the wall by a small angle brace. However, first place double-faced foam tape on the underside of the corners of the bottom frames so they will not move. Do this after the panels are in place; use a crowbar to lift the panel.

Figure 41   Freestanding Panels

Freestanding panels are attached and placed in a geometric pattern to support one another, such as four panels making a square and three creating an equilateral triangle. Both shapes form a kiosk on which to display graphics, framed objects and label copy. An opening cut in the side allows for an exhibit case. Another alternative is a 90° zigzag arrangement in which a group of three to six or more panels are connected in an undulating wall. The zigzag units, of course, need to have sheeting material such as plywood, Upsom board or hardboard on both sides of the 1x4″ frames.

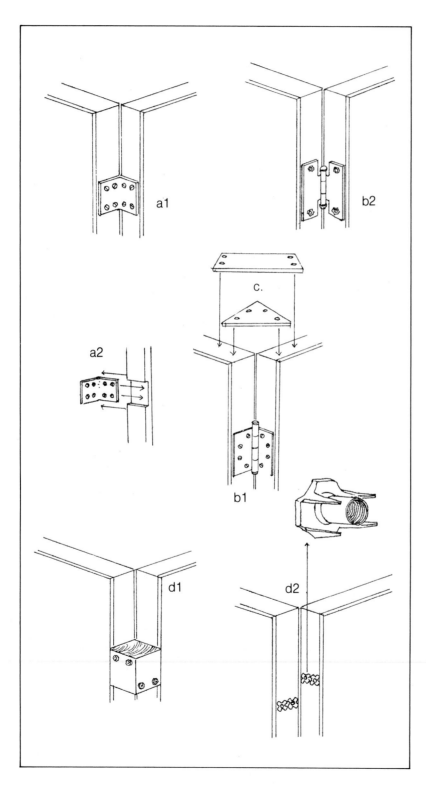

Figure 42   Corner Braces

The connecting devices for all freestanding units are corner braces (angle irons) either mounted directly on the 1x4" pine frame (a1) or sunk flush in a rectangular groove, or dado, (a2) carved beforehand. Connectors need not be concealed if they are well made and neat; they can give the appearance of design details. Chrome, brass or a black matte finish are very attractive. You might even consider oversized screw heads for accent. Besides a corner brace to secure the panels, you might want a hinge connector (b1 and b2). Regardless of the hinge size, a locking device on the top will prevent the two panels from spreading beyond the display angle of 90°. A triangular gusset plate or even a long mending plate (c) will do the job. Another connector to consider is a 4" square block of wood (d1) with eight pre-drilled holes. Corresponding holes with "Tee-nuts" are set at each point (d2) on the panel frame to fit the wood block connector. This is an extremely flexible system especially if you intend to use the panels again and again. Tee-nuts and other threaded inserts used in wood have a machine thread that take a bolt in the inside. These inserts come in many sizes.

Figure 43   Mending Plates

Panels can be fastened together at the back with strap irons or mending plates, leaving the fronts clear of any obvious connectors. Since metal mending plates are straight, put them in a vise and bend them to the desired angle with a pair of pliers (a). A second method is to cut triangular pieces of wood and "toe" them into the frames (b); a third is to screw a mending plate in at the top of two adjoining frames. Zigzag panels can be bolted to the wall at either end with angle braces (c).

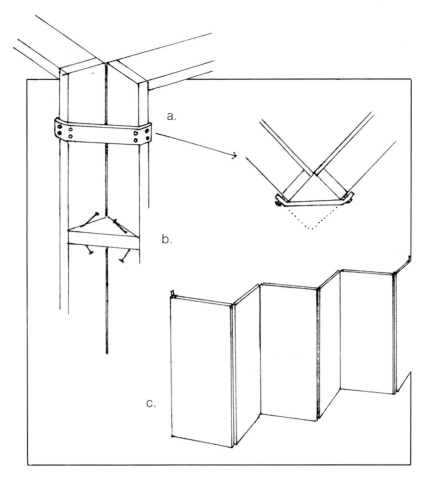

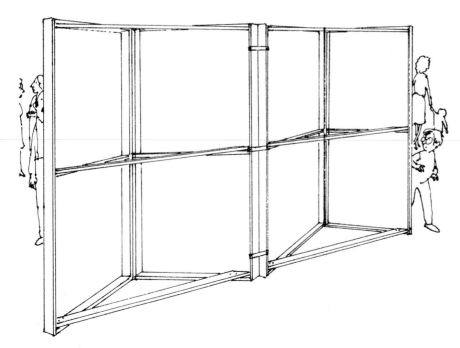

Figure 44   Further Bracing

If they cannot be fastened to a wall, zigzag panels can be additionally stabilized by screwing in 1x4" pieces of lumber horizontally across the back from vertical frame to vertical frame.

Figure 45   Bolts and Angle Irons

For an arrangement of panels standing flat against a wall, prepare them as suggested earlier, and lay them face down on the floor with their base braced against the wall. Drill ¼" holes through the two vertical frames at approximately 2' intervals so that they can be bolted together. Do all the drilling while the panels are flat on the floor. Bolt two pairs of panels together; then lift them up and bolt those pairs to other pairs. You will need a number of helpers for this task, most to hold the panels upright while one person attaches the bolts and nuts. After the panels have been fastened together, gently move into position against the wall.

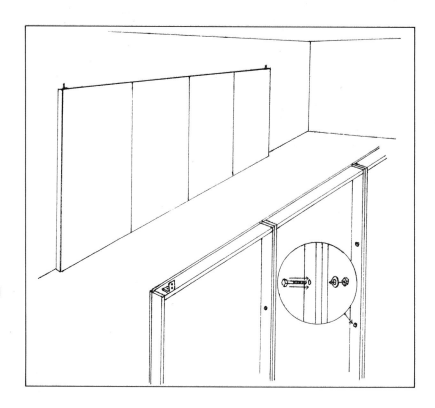

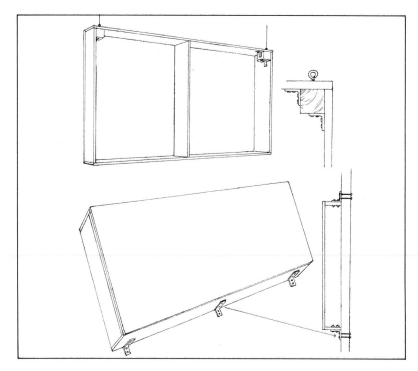

Figure 46   Braided Picture Wire or Braces

Braided picture wire and eyebolts are used to hang 4x8' horizontal panels on the wall (a). Make sure both are strong enough to support heavy weight. Use double-faced foam tape on the rear corners of the panel to prevent it from swinging. The panel and its contents will be more secure, however, if you fasten it directly onto the wall. The simplest technique is to mount the panel to the wall with corner braces (b). First screw the braces to the wall, lining them up with a board and carpenter's level. Additional braces can be added in between if the panel is very heavy. Set the panel onto the braces. They can also be attached to the bottom frame.

Figure 47   Gravity Wedge

A strong hanging device concealed from view is a gravity wedge, or cleat. Wedge-shaped blocks hold the panel and its contents firmly in place by the force of gravity. The 4′ gripping assembly is glued and screwed into back of panel (a). The finished assembly should be 3⅝″ wide and extend ⅛″ beyond frame of panel (b). The block attached to the panel, left, fits over one screwed into the wall, right (c). See page xx for proper anchors in wall. To prevent shifting of the panel, attach small (about 1″) squares of double-faced foam tape to the two lower corners of the frame and push panel tight to the wall.

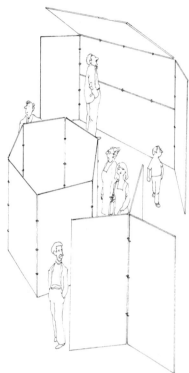

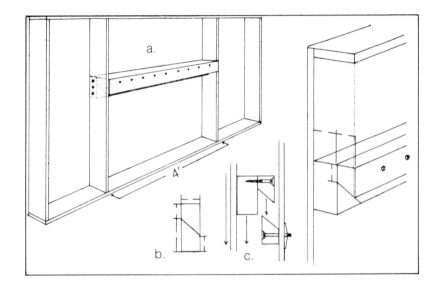

Figure 48   Klem Fasteners

Finally, one of the simplest panel-connecting systems is the use of Klem fasteners to clip together ¾″, 4x8′ chip board or plywood sheets with a painted or natural finish. See page 54 for information on Klem fasteners.

Figure 49   Keyhole Plate

Another device that cannot be seen is the "keyhole plate" fastened to the back of the panel. This attachment method is excellent for a small panel. It rests on strong anchors and protruding screw heads in the wall. In the detail shown at lower right, the 2x4 has an area routed to a depth (a) of the thickness of the plate, and (b) to accommodate the screw head. These plates come in various sizes; make sure you use the right one. When the panel is hung, secure the bottom corners with tape.

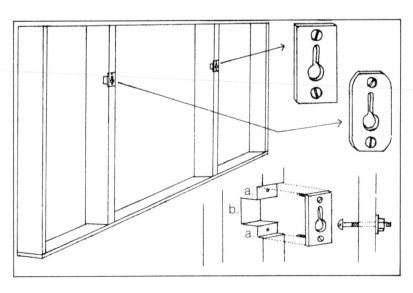

■ Case Construction

Cases are transparent containers in which objects are placed for protection. Their shape and size is determined by the object that is to be placed inside. One could write a separate volume just to discuss the variety of cases used in museums around the world today. However, for this guide, we will discuss only a few simple designs and their fabrication that can be used for objects in a traveling exhibition. Old cases may also be remodeled for a more contemporary look. (See Arminta Neal, *Help for the Small Museum,* Pruett Press, 1969, Boulder, Co.)

The easiest case to make consists of four sheets of glass clamped together with Klem fasteners

Figure 50   Case 1

A case easy to erect consists of four sheets of 4x8' glass joined together with Klem fasteners and mounted on a base. It can house a single large pedestal or a group in various sizes (e). Fabrics can be draped on a dowel frame (a). Spacing bars of 1x2" are secured at the top (b). A base of 2x4' has mitered corners that are glued and screwed (d). Sheets of glass rest in a groove cut ⅜" wide and ½" deep (c).

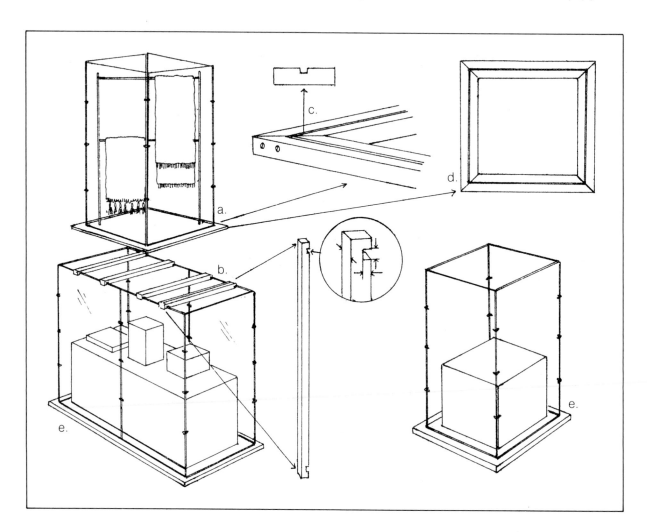

(Case 1, Figure 50). A large case of this type, 4′ wide and up to 12′ long, will enclose a tableau of costumed mannequins. However, it must be noted that this case is not dust tight. It is recommended only for protecting objects from damage, theft, or the touch of viewers.

Another simple solution is a box case on legs standing behind the window of a standard 4x8′ panel (Case 2, Figure 51). The other sides are solid (if placed against a wall only two are needed), and attached by 1x4″ braces. To make the case virtually dust tight, glue felt strips or a rubber gasket around the front.

Case 3 is the standard box configuration for mounting on a panel or on a wall. Two of these can be placed back to back on a pedestal. Their

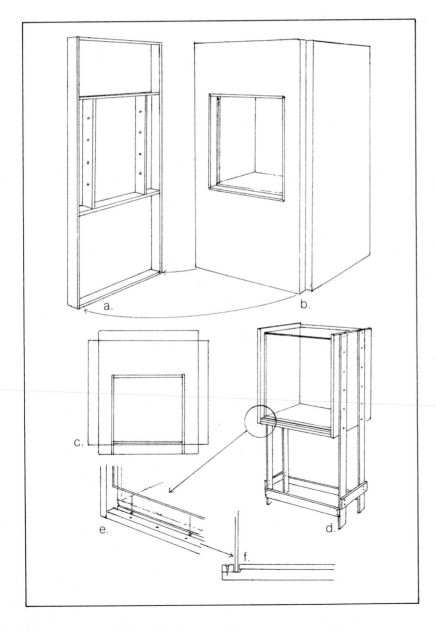

a.   b.

c.

e.

f.

d.

Figure 51   Case 2

For a case of simple construction, an opening is cut into a 4x8′ wood panel (a). Solid panels of the same size are added to surround the display case (b). An overhead plan view indicates the position of the case inside the panels (c). It is built of ¾″ plywood mounted on legs to fit into the panel opening (d). After objects are installed, the case is closed with ¼″ plate glass (or plastic) held firm with wooden molding screwed down in front (e). The glass sits in the rabbeted front edge of box (f). An additional strip of molding may be necessary to cover cracks between case and panel.

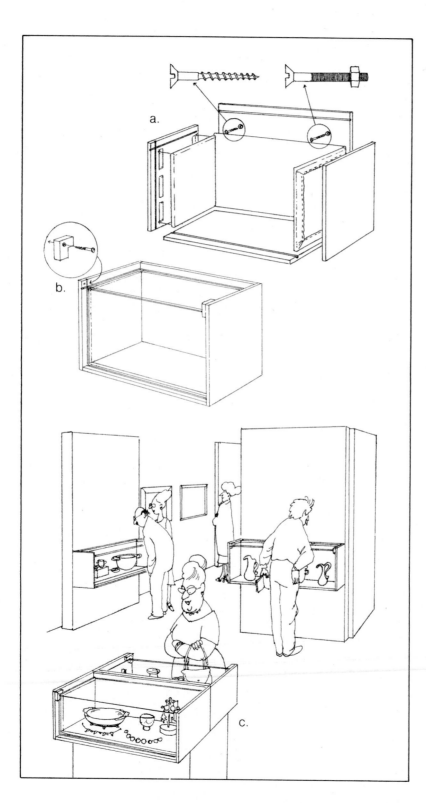

Figure 52   Case 3

A simple rectangular case of glass and wood can be bolted to a panel (equipped with extra interior bracing) or to a wall. The bolts in the back are countersunk (a), and hidden by cloth-covered or veneered panels attached to the interior with double-faced tape. Glass or plastic sheets are slid into dado cuts, front sheet first. The case is locked with a hardwood notched block, screwed into place at the top front corners (b). Two units may be placed back to back on a block pedestal to form a freestanding table case (c).

Figure 53   Case 4

Plexiglas cubes can be installed on your own pedestals and bases. Fasten them securely with screws.

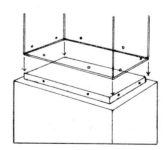

shape can vary from shallow and high to long and deep.

Of course, cases may be purchased ready made from a display house. The least expensive version, which requires you and your assistants to do half the work, is the Plexiglas cube. These plastic units will last quite a few years if they are carefully maintained while in use and properly wrapped when stored. We recommend that you develop a modular system of measurements, as with all your exhibit furniture (panels, pedestals) that will allow for repeated use. Other types of

cases that you can assemble yourself will be discussed in the sections on Structural Systems and Commercial Structural Systems.

□ *Finishing*

The design and color scheme will be determined by the theme and type of exhibit you are planning. If you decide to paint, a first grade plywood with an interesting grain pattern is not necessary. A second grade wood will suffice. The best paint finish on cases is a matte lacquer that will withstand tremendous punishment from the public. Lacquer must be sprayed, so if you do not have in-house capabilities, consult with an exhibit display house or an auto repair shop with spraying equipment to see if they would be willing to undertake the spray painting of your cases. If these sources are not available, paint the cases yourself with a brush and a top grade paint that can be washed periodically. An alternative is a natural wood finish. If that is your choice, make sure that you use a first grade plywood with a

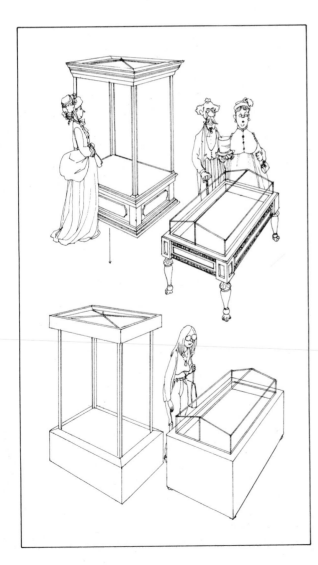

Figure 54   New Look for an Old Case

If an exhibition has a slick contemporary look the insertion of antique cases could be a visual jolt, and may truly detract from the objects to be displayed. If so, make "skirts" out of Upsom board, plywood, or hardboard, properly framed, to hide piano legs or intricately carved mahogany or oak bases. (For details, see Arminta Neal's book, *Help for the Small Museum.*) Fabricate the skirts in such a manner that they can be removed without damage. You may at some future date install an exhibition in which antique cases might add just the right touch for a true *period* feeling; besides, many old exhibit cases are works of art in themselves.

hardwood veneer to match other natural finishes in your gallery. Whatever you choose, remember that maintenance is an important consideration. You do not want a finish that will not last through the run of the exhibition.

□ *Connecting and Mounting Devices*
Both the gravity wedge or cleat and the keyhole plate shown in Figures 47 and 49 can be used also to mount exhibit cases. These techniques, however, are not the best for high-traffic areas where jolting and jostling crowds could dislodge a case. It is much safer to bolt it directly to a well-braced panel or to a wall using heavy-duty anchors. (See page 48 for details on attaching to hollow surfaces and solid surfaces.)

Figure 55   Gravity Wedge

The gravity wedge can also be employed to fasten double-faced panels together. Accurate measurements and good craftsmanship are essential for this technique.

■ Matting and Framing

If you have unmounted photographs, prints, drawings, watercolors or manuscript pages but are without an experienced framer on hand (or if you want to save money) then you will have to do the work yourself.

Check with an art supply store to make sure it has mat board and backing board made of 100 percent rag (with neutral ph) as well as archival corner mounts that are acid free. If not, contact the sources on page 161 for archival presentation and preservation supplies. Besides the mounting board, mat board and corner mounts, you should have a mat cutter, metal straight edge, mat knife, ruler and pencil. It is important to use materials that will not harm the art. Too much shabby and careless work, not to mention ignorance, in the past has damaged too many valuable archival and art objects.

As you set to work, prepare two clean tables—one on which to cut the board and another to hold the graphics, which should be protected with tissue. On a sheet of paper, identify, number and note the actual size as well as the frame size, of each. If you plan to display a group of objects, make all the frames one standard size. If there are a few larger objects, select two standard sizes. To determine the frame sizes, find the largest and smallest items. The margins for the largest should measure a minimum of 2½" at each side, 3½" at the bottom and 3" at the top.

Pre-cut metal and wood frame kits are probably available from an art supply or hardware store. If you use these, adjust your margins to the closest pre-cut size. If not, you will have to buy wood molding at a lumberyard and glass at a hardware store in order to make the frames yourself.

Cut one sample backing board to size and carefully lay the largest and the smallest objects on the board to see how they look, taking into account that a mat will cover an edge of about 1/16" to ⅛". If the mat board window looks too small or too large for some objects, you may want to change the size of the frame.

A simple narrow molding for your frames looks best; however, it should be strong enough to hold

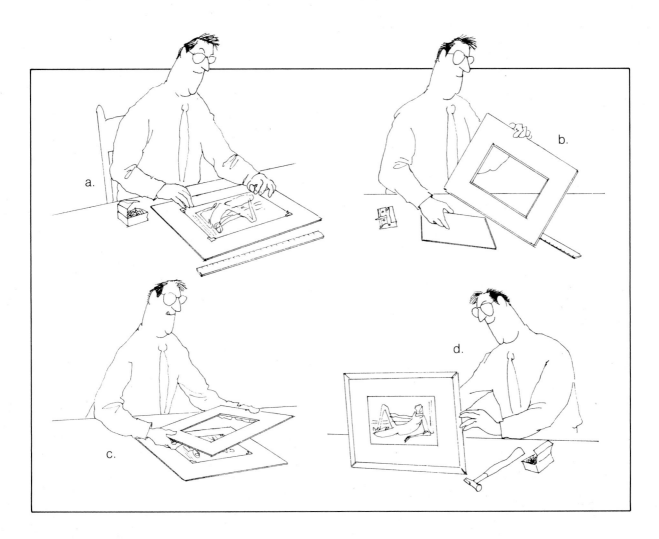

Figure 56   How to Mat and Mount a Picture

Lay the watercolor, print or drawing on the backing board where you think it looks best. Mark the board lightly with pencil; then measure and center the work exactly. Affix an archival corner mount on the board at each corner; let dry and carefully insert the art into the mounts (a). The fit should not be tight. When the picture is securely fastened to the backing board, measure again and note these measurements in light pencil on the mat board; remember to leave a slight margin to cover the archival corner mounts. Now, using the metal straight edge as a guide, cut the window (b). Erase any pencil lines and place the mat on top of the backing board. If you have measured and cut correctly, the art work should be in the right position (c). While the cutting and mounting is taking place, another person can be assembling the frames, cutting glass and finishing the wood. If you use a metal frame, it can be assembled and the glass cleaned so it is ready to place on the matted art work (d).

the weight of the glass. A uniform frame size for all of your works will facilitate the installation of the exhibition.

   When you decide upon the frame size, start cutting the backing and mat boards. Cut with the mat knife, using the metal straight edge, and make sure the corners are square. Stack the mat boards in one pile and the backing boards in another. Mounting of this type does require skill and should be done by a person of experience. Figure 55 explains the correct technique for matting and framing.

■ Hanging Devices

A problem faced by most museum people is to find a practical and convenient method of mounting the exhibit. You will be happy to know that there are no simple and easy solutions. Each exhibit brings with it its unique qualities as well as its unique problems. All exhibits share this trait. Careful planning, patience, hard work, and attention to detail is the only approach.

The most frequently asked question by smaller institutions requesting assistance in the installation is, "What is the simplest and best way to secure an object to the wall?" We have discussed a number of solutions as they pertain to large panels and to wall-hung exhibit cases; that is, by drilling into the wall itself and placing anchors (see page 48). Here are some additional methods.

□ *Picture Rods*
A simple method is the picture rod shown in Figure 57. It comes in various lengths and has a spring-lock or cam-lock hook that can be raised or lowered on the rod. To this hook you attach one corner of a framed object or panel, via a screw eye; the hook is then securely locked. Two picture rods are used for each object. They can be painted to match your wall color.

□ *Wire and Cable*
A second method, braided picture wire, used with hooks attached to a wall molding, has been a time-tested method for hanging paintings, framed graphics and panels (Figure 58). Here you will have to use a ladder to place the hooks on the molding, attach lengths of wire to the hooks and then attach the wires to the frame. The gauge of braided wire must have the tensile strength to safely support the painting.

The biggest problem here is to insure that your object is hung level and at the right height. Braided wire will stretch according to the weight

Figure 57   Picture Rods

Picture rods are a good device for hanging paintings and small panels without putting holes in the walls. These steel or iron rods, usually about ⅜" square in cross section, have a hook at the top to fit over a strip of wall molding. (Better known as "picture rail," wall molding is generally a soft pine strip nailed close to the ceiling to support heavy duty picture hooks.)

of the object—the heavier the object and the larger the wire, the greater is the stretch. So hanging any object or group of objects successfully by this method will take trial and error until you master the technique.

Some museums are now using "airplane cable" made of strong alloy wires that are braided (Figure 58c). It will not stretch and has an extremely high tensile strength. This cable is expensive but if available at your hardware store, give it a try.

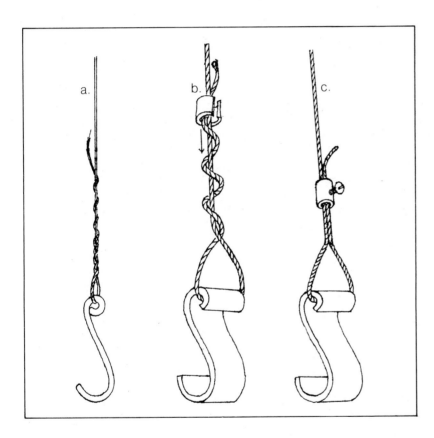

Figure 58 Wire and Cable

Braided picture wire is looped around the bottom of the hook and twisted back into itself (a). Then a lead crimp is used to hold the wire in place and prevent it from unraveling or slipping; the crimp is squeezed firmly with pliers (b). The bottom of the wire is attached to a screw eye on the back of a frame or on the top of a panel. Looped cable is twisted by using a special cable crimp with a set screw; when tightened, it will engage the loose end of the cable and hold it securely (c).

□ *Rope*

Rope as a material for hanging an exhibition has obvious limitations such as its lack of elegance. However, where it is appropriate—as for instance in a show of farm implements, crafts or a nautical subject—rope, knots and all of its wonderful hardware like pulleys, cleats and hooks could be put to good use. The danger there lies in overdoing the rustic approach, so moderation is advisable. If used judiciously, however, rope can be an effective, functional and decorative material. The hardware can be purchased at a farm supply/hardware store or a marine supply store.

□ *Double–Faced Tape*

Much has been said already about double-faced tape and its uses. This material has been one of the most convenient aids in exhibit preparation since its arrival on the market a number of years ago. The industrial version of this product, the best known being 3M double-faced foam tape, is being used by many museum technicians across the country for a variety of tasks and is particularly useful for securing display furnishings. Easily obtainable at hardware stores, it should be included in the tool kit of every museum. However there are several caveats. Extreme caution is advisable in the use of this product for securing or holding objects. The chemical composition of the tape may have deleterious effects on many materials such as glass, ceramics, paper and paper products, leather, wood and metal. It is therefore best not to bring it in direct contact with exhibit objects, at least not without previously consulting with the lender, oranizer or a conservator.

A further word of caution is offered regarding foam tape applied to and left on a painted surface for more than two months. Paint may lift off with it when finally removed. A slight residue may be left on any surface that has been attached with the tape. Be very careful, therefore, when removing it. If a slight residue is left on the surface, dip a clean cloth in a solvent (paint thinner, rubber cement thinner, or even lighter fluid), test its effect on the surface in a small area and if satisfied, wipe off the residue. The primary purpose of this tape is to secure small pedestals and mounts in cases. It is also handy for mounting labels on a vertical surface, and small mirrors in a case where the back or base of an object is to be made visible to the viewer.

Foam tape can be used on the floor to secure pedestals to prevent them from shifting if suddenly bumped. In this case, long lengths should be affixed to all underside edges of the pedestal. It can also be attached to the bottom corners of panels, exhibit systems and freestanding structures.

On the wall, small squares of tape can be placed on the lower corners of a frame or panel. Label panels of cardboard, hardboard, thin plywood or foamcore can be mounted with tape directly on a wall or a larger panel, but you must be prepared that this will leave a mark when removed.

□ *Fastening to Solid and Hollow Surfaces*
If a wall is of solid construction (concrete, concrete block, or brick covered with plaster) it is sound for anchoring. Using a variable speed electric hand drill fitted with a carbide-tipped drill bit is the easiest way to penetrate solid walls.

For attaching light weights up to one hundred pounds per fastener you can use a screw to attach your bracket or angle iron to the wall (Figure 59a and b). For heavy objects, use a masonry bolt. It is available in different sizes and head types, including hooks, screw eyes and threaded ends that accept nuts.

For walls that are hollow, a variety of fasteners can be used, including the gravity toggle (Figure

Figure 59   Solid Walls

Two methods are used for attaching lightweight objects. The first is to drill a hole up to ½" in diameter and a depth of 1½" to 2". Hammer a slightly oversized wooden dowel into the hole until it is flush (a). Next drill a pilot hole into the center of the dowel, slightly smaller than the screw. Use a screw with a washer to attach your bracket, angle iron or corner brace to the wall. The second method is to take a wall plug of fiber, plastic or lead and hammer into the pre-drilled hole (b). Turn the screw about one-quarter of the way in (causing the plug to expand in the hole) and then unscrew it. Slip the screw through the object being fastened and drive the screw home. (Note: Do not overtighten since too much pressure may start your plug to rotate and you will then have a loose connection.) For heavy objects, use a masonry bolt instead of the plugs (c). This has a plastic or sometimes lead sheath that expands as the bolt is threaded into the hole. Drill a hole, as with the plugs, to the proper size opening to receive the bolt and its sheath.

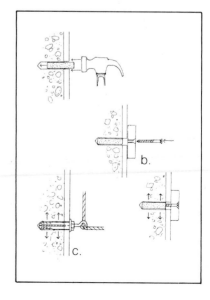

Figure 60   Hollow Walls

To attach the gravity and split-wing bolts, drill a hole with a carbide drill bit large enough to pass through the bolt and collapsed toggle or split-wing toggle (a & b). Before pushing the assembly through the hole, unscrew the bolt from the assembly, pass the bolt through your angle iron or corner brace, rescrew the bolt to the toggle. Then push the assembly into the hole. For the collapsible anchor or molly bolt (c), drill a passage for the assembly to pass through snugly, tighten the bolt until pressure is felt (as the bolt is turned, it draws the metal-gripping shoulders up against the inner wall), remove the bolt by unscrewing it (the anchor remains in place as the bolt is removed), pass the bolt through your angle iron and rescrew the bolt into the anchor until tight.

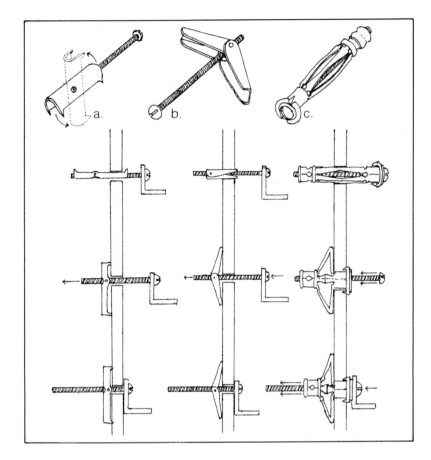

60a), split-wing toggle bolt (Figure 60b) and collapsible anchor or molly bolt (Figure 60c). Heavy objects on a hollow wall require a different device. Here it is advisable to create a bridge made of lumber fastened to interior wall studs by using a lag screw to fasten the lumber cross member up against the wall. You can then attach your object to the cross member. Studs are usually 16″ apart, center to center, but check with the building superintendent to confirm this. Locate the studs by tapping the wall or probe for them by drilling with a ¹⁄₁₆″ drill bit near the baseboard.

■ **Structural Systems**

If you are engaged in a temporary exhibition program, you will sooner or later need some kind of structural system on which to mount your

exhibit. The exclusive use of framed panels, either freestanding or wall mounted, is satisfactory but they can be cumbersome and may present a storage problem. Also, panels alone do not provide for versatility in presentation. They are neutral, which on occasion may be desirable, but generally a mixture of large panels and a flexible structural system is preferable.

An ideal gallery space should have the following features: wall surface of plywood paneling, either cloth covered or painted, to which elements could easily be attached; picture molding for hanging; and flexible panel and structural systems with provisions to create exhibit cases.

We mention this only in passing as something to think about. Perhaps planning and good fortune in finding a donor might eventually afford you to create the perfect gallery space. If budget

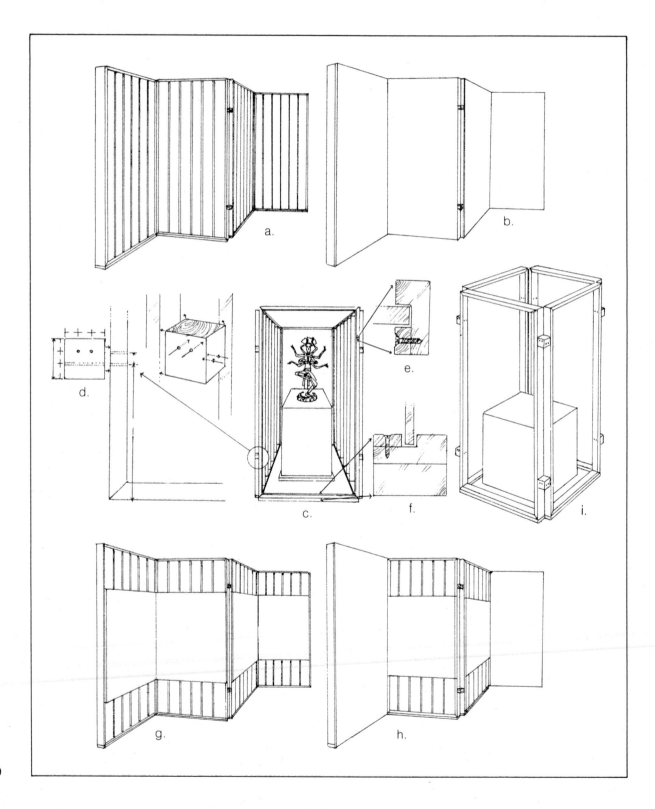

Figure 61 2x4 Panel System

a. A typical 2x4 wood panel system 8' high, used as a "see-through" barrier. Openings between the vertical 2x4s measure 6¼".
b. Panel system covered with 4x8' sheets form a "solid" wall.
c. Case made of the basic 2x4 system with front panel of glass.

Back is a solid panel and the sides are "see-through" vertical 2x4s.
d. A 3½" square block, end grain up, is used as connector for right angle assembly. Pilot holes are drilled ³/₁₆" wide and 1" on all four sides.
e. and f. Typical frame to accommodate a 4x8' sheet of ¼" plate glass (trimmed to

3'10"x7'10"). Screw is countersunk. Notch is lined with felt strips.
g. Basic panel system with 4x4' plywood sheets.
h. A mix of 4x4' and 4x8' sheets.
i. Lumber frames size 2x4 step-cut (called rabbeting) with 4x8' sheets of glass will form enclosures that can be used as large exhibit cases.

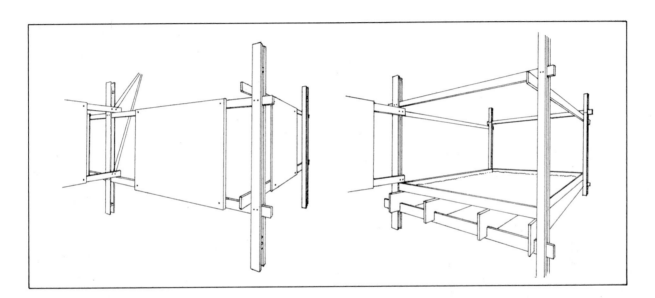

Figure 62 Boards and Bolts

Another simple wood system is made of 1x4" lumber and bolted together to form vertical and horizontal members. Tee-nuts are inserted for end grain connection (X). Painted or

cloth-covered panels are bolted back to back through 1x4" frames. At the top and bottom of each vertical member, 1x4x4" blocks are glued into place. Foam tape under the legs will insure that the unit does not "skip" on the floor when jostled.

This is designed to accommodate flat graphics and framed objects. For three-dimensional articles, a platform can be constructed in the same style using 1x4" lumber; however, it is not appropriate for an exhibition with tight security.

is a problem and you wish to have a structural system, you may have to build your own until you can afford one that is commercially made. If you, your staff, your volunteers or talented resource persons can design and build your own system that works, here are some suggestions for such a project (see Figures 61 and 62).

□ **Wood**
The easiest material to work with is wood. It is plentiful and it lends itself nicely as a structural element. Wood units, however, tend to be heavy since vertical risers and horizontal bracing must be sufficiently bulky in order to be structurally sound. Also, with the continuing rise in lumber

Figure 63   Spider Unit

A three-armed connector located at the tops and bottoms of three panels forms a "spider unit." The panels are standard 1x4" plywood double-faced with 3x8' sheeting. The three-armed connector is made of 1x4" lumber held together with wrought iron flange plates. Pins are used to join the connector to the panels. Iron plates are welded in a metal shop.

Figure 64   Modular Cube

A 3' square cube system is made of 2x⅞" dressed lumber and panels of Plexiglas and plywood (a). Each unit is constructed of 12 pieces of wood cut 3' long and fastened together with screws (all screw holes are in the identical location) (b). Each 3' unit can be connected horizontally or stacked vertically (c) with a ⅜" diameter hardwood dowel, 1½" long (½" deep dowel holes are located at each connecting corner point). The protruding dowels also act as connectors for Plexiglas covers measuring 3x3', so each cube is a small exhibit case. When stacked, there is a ½" clearance between vertical members; this space can be taken up with a ¼" plywood panel for an opaque shelf (d), or a ¼" Plexiglas panel for a transparent shelf (e).

For this system to work, accurate measurements and fine craftsmanship are necessary because of extremely close tolerance. We suggest that a jig be developed for all cutting of the lumber as well as for the drilling of holes. We recommend that a pine prototype be fabricated first to work out the details. If you can afford it, a hardwood would be ideal. As long as the tools are sharp, these woods can be cut and drilled as successfully as softwoods. The structure should be finished in fine natural wood.

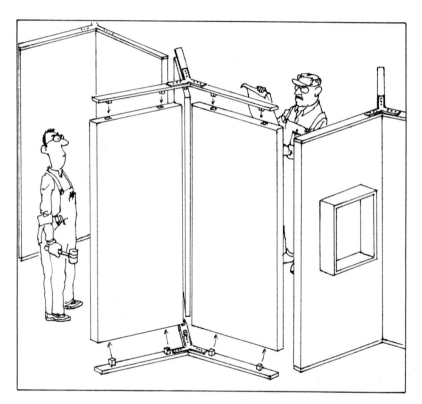

prices, you should think twice and carefully evaluate what you need, what will provide the greatest flexibility and, finally, what the end cost will be. Should you decide to fabricate your own system, whether of wood or any other substance, prepare a few designs along with detailed drawings, make a list of quantities, and obtain estimates on the raw materials and hardware that would be required to construct the systems. You can then judge if the time and expenditure for each will be satisfactory. It may be worthwhile to compare prices with commercially available systems.

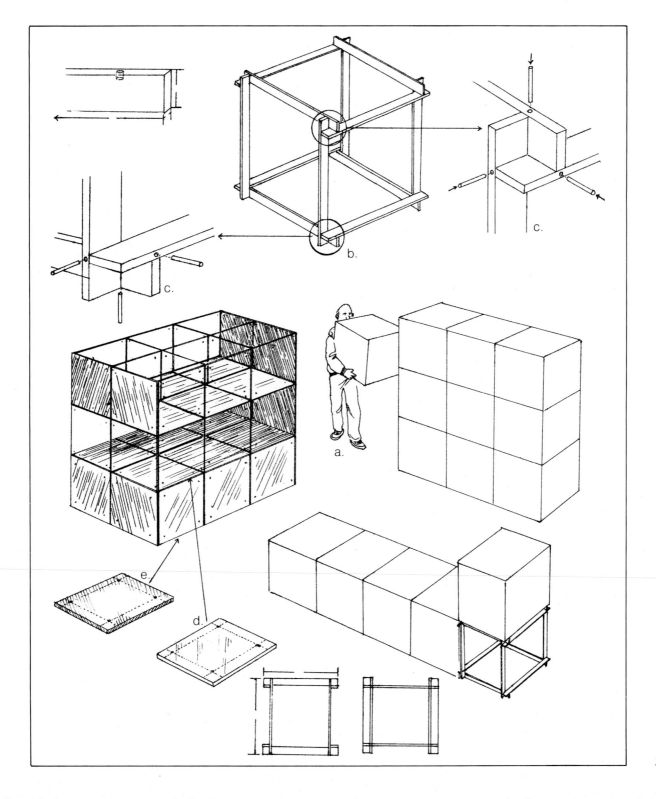

Figure 65   Klem Fastener

The versatile Klem fastener can be used to clamp panels up to ¾" thick to a vertical pipe or tube having a 1" outside diameter. Remember to set up such a structure in a geometric configuration in order to establish stability. (See page 160 for source.)

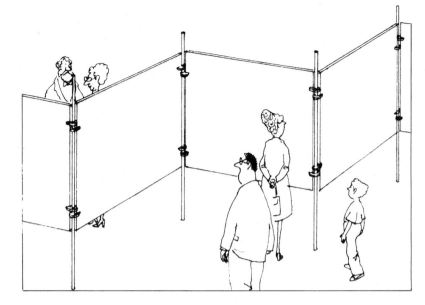

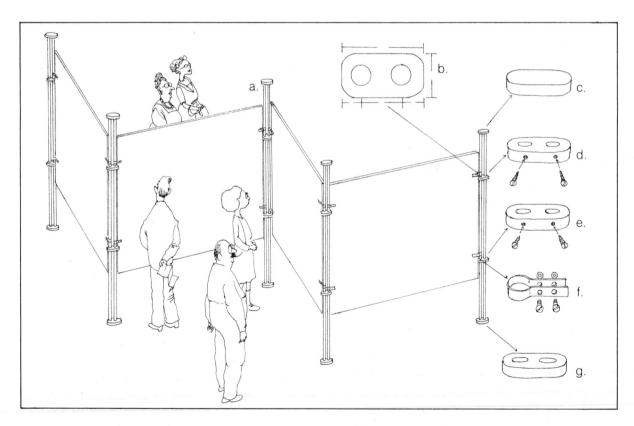

Figure 66   Clamp and Anchor

A ¾" plywood or chip board panel is mounted on a 1" tube or pipe (a). Two ⅜" panels can also be placed back to back. The hardwood anchor contains holes 1" in diameter (b). Wood cap (c) and base (g) are identical. Holes are only ½" deep. Metal set screws are inserted at side (d & e). Clamp of 1" strap iron is bolted through panel (f).

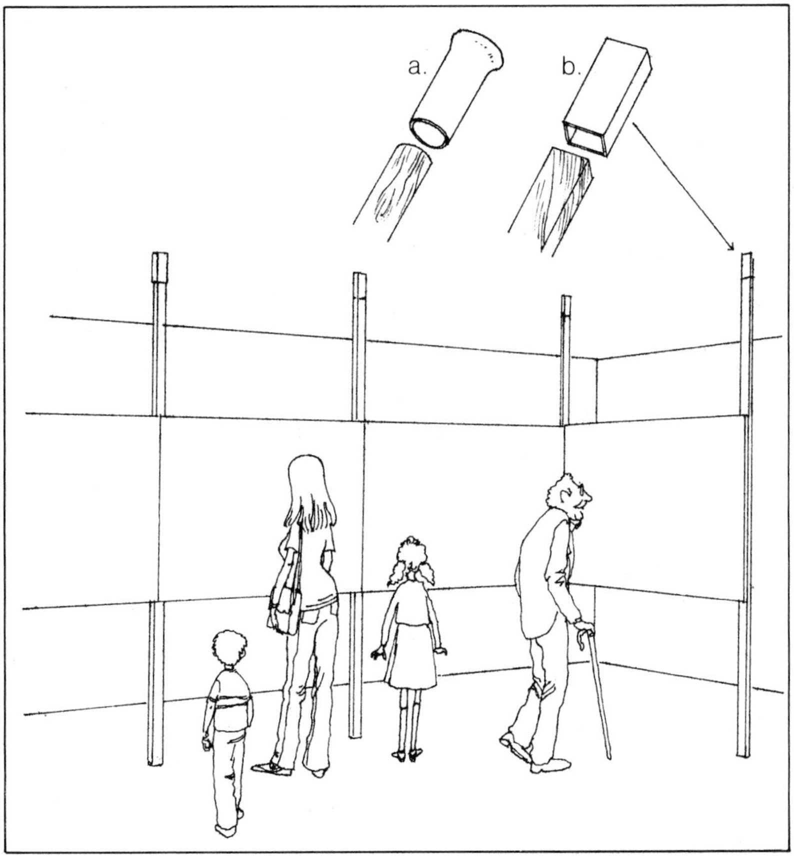

Figure 67   Timber-Topper

A rectangular 8″-long steel sleeve fits over the end of a standard "dressed" 2x4 available at all lumberyards. The sleeve contains a strong spring and when compressed and moved into place securely holds the 2x4 in a vertical position, even with panels attached. Another version, which is round, fits a standard 1⅝″ diameter closet pole, pipe or tube. The round sleeve is 7″ long and made of birch or maple that can be left natural. Drawing (a) illustrates the round sleeve; drawing (b) the rectangular. (See page 160 for source.)

□ Pipe and Tube

A few examples of pipe and tube usage have been illustrated on page 54. Figure 65 shows the Klem fastener method and Figure 66 connectors you can make out of wood, strap metal and pipe. Hardware stores stock a variety of pipe and tube devices that might be adaptable for gallery use.

□ Compression

A simple compression system is the "Timber-Topper" shown in Figure 67. This device requires a ceiling strong enough to withstand the tension. A hung acoustical ceiling, for example, will not do; it must be solid. For a secure installation the ceiling height should be between 8 and 10 feet. A ceiling over 10 or 11 feet is too high to accommodate the poles, since the vertical supports lose their rigidity as their height increases. You can

get bending and a "whip-like" action if you accidentally strike the vertical pole.

□ Pedestals and Risers

You will always need a selection of pedestals and risers to use with your exhibit installations. There often occurs a strange phenomenon—regardless of how many pedestals of different shapes and sizes are in storage in a museum, you will invariably need one in the size and shape you do not have. So do not despair, you are not alone.

If you have developed a system of modular panels and exhibit cases, you need a selection of pedestals and risers to match. They should be built with solid sides to give greater flexibility (Figure 68). Large risers for displaying furniture should have open bottoms, otherwise they will be too heavy to be moved around.

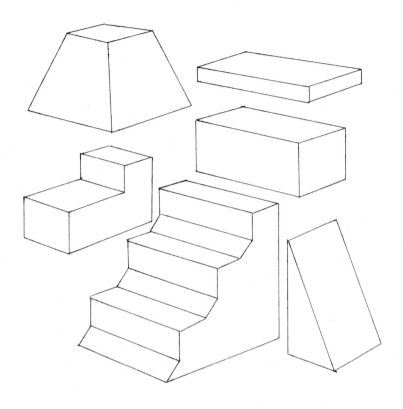

Figure 68 Freestanding Pedestals

A pedestal should be solid, with all six faces covered, so it can be placed on its side (a). It should be made of ½" plywood, edges mitered (b). Interior glue blocks are glued and nailed into place. Nails are countersunk with a nail set, their holes filled and sanded.

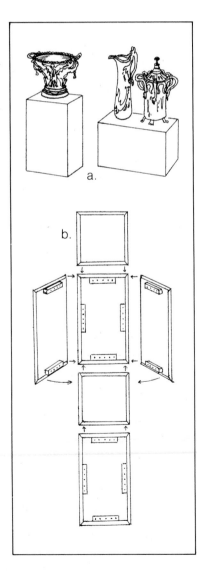

a.

b.

Figure 69 Pedestals and Risers

Case furniture can be made of ⅜" Upsom board, ½"-thick Homosote, or ¼ or ⅜" plywood. Cuts must be accurate since the finished product will be viewed at close range.

Figure 70 A Glass Shelf

Glass is a material effectively used for certain types of objects; a sheet can be set on one or more blocks to form a riser on which to display antique silver or porcelain.

Figure 71 Circular Stand

To make a round shape, cut out three circles, notch and fasten to three or four vertical 1x1" braces. Wrap the frame with ⅛" Upsom board (Easy-Curve) tacked with brads and glued at the vertical braces.

Heavier pedestals are more stable and less likely to tip over; double-faced foam tape on the underside of the pedestal will give even greater stability. Place the pedestals in their final location, then attach the tape. Set the object on the pedestals. It might be necessary to screw little padded "Z" plates into the pedestal top to secure the object (see page 102). Some museums use a removable side panel (attached with screws that are painted) so that a heavy weight can be placed inside for stability.

Pedestals that will stand behind glass or a barrier can have a lighter construction of ½" homosote, ½" plywood or ⅜" Upsom board, with interior glue blocks. The entire box is glued and nailed with brads (nailheads are countersunk and filled), sanded and painted.

For a cloth-covered pedestal, it is best to wrap the material around a thin panel such as ⅛" hardboard with mitered edges. Pull the cloth taut and glue it on the back, holding it in place with tape while it dries. Finishing nails carefully driven through pilot holes and using a nail set will attach cloth-covered panels to the pedestal; the cloth will hide the finishing nails. The top cloth-covered panel is placed last. If executed with good craftsmanship, this treatment can look quite elegant.

□ *Furniture for Case Interiors*
A collection of small pedestals, boxes and small risers is necessary to support objects inside the cases. Simple rectangular and square forms are the most practical. The choice of a finish will depend upon the material to be displayed. (For an ethnographic exhibit, or one dealing with antique farm implements, rough blocks of wood would be appropriate.) With your mock-up of each case, as described on page 7, you can determine the number and sizes of furniture required for the exhibition. The fabrication will be easier if you standardize your sizes to four to six different shapes. Arrange for an accurate count of your needs.

Pedestals can be finished to match the case interior. For a special effect, cover them with mirrors, using contact cement, hot glue or even double-faced foam tape (see page 153 for glass cutting). The case furniture should never predominate but only show off the objects to best advantage. Beware of raw edges, wrinkled cloth, finger marks or smudges.

Storage is a problem. In order to keep track of storage items keep an inventory list of the items and their sizes. Note also their location, condition, covering and most recent coat of paint (color and type). Small pieces should be wrapped and packed in a carton, marked on the outside. All of this may seem a bit fussy, but it will save you time and effort later on.

■ Commercial Structural Systems

There are a number of commercial structural systems on the market that can save you endless hours of work and frustration. The main problem is that they are generally expensive. Most of the systems listed here have been around for a number of years and have been found satisfactory by institutions using them. Also, they are "modular," and can be added to as funds are available.

When you decide upon a system, stick with it. None is interchangeable unless you have a limitless budget and want to invest in a variety of complete systems. Check into all that are available to see what they can and cannot do. Consider them in relation to your own needs—the nature of exhibits you plan to show, floor space and ceiling height of your gallery, storage space, turnover time for the next exhibit, and the amount of manpower available.

With a flexible modular unit at your disposal, the installations will be easier to plan and fabricate. One real problem is that your exhibits may start to look alike unless you use some imagination in the arrangement, color and lighting.

When selecting a commercial system, remember that it should not dominate so that all you see is structure. It should be secondary to the objects on exhibit—provide only an unobtrusive setting, quiet and functional.

We are listing a number of systems (selected by the author) and their characteristics to aid you in the selection process.

57

Commercial Structural Systems Chart

System*	System Abstracta Fig. 72	Alka Structures Fig. 73	Apton System Fig. 74
Basic Description	Steel tube and connector structural system	Extruded aluminum tubes and spring lock system	Square 1″ tube and connector system
Structure only	Yes	Yes	Yes
Panels only	No	No	No
Client supplies panels	Yes	Yes	Yes
Complete system	No	No	No
Can create exhibit cases	Yes	Yes	Yes
Structural versatility	Excellent	Excellent	Excellent
Has its own lighting system	Yes	None	None
Durability of parts	Excellent	Good to excellent	Excellent
Ease of assembly	Excellent	Fair to good	Excellent
Ease of disassembly	Excellent	Good	Excellent
Strength and stability	Excellent	Excellent	Excellent
Appearance	Excellent	Good to excellent	Good to excellent
Weight of system	Medium	Heavy to medium	Heavy to medium
Compactness of storage	Excellent	Good to excellent	Excellent
Accessories	Varied	Varied	Varied
Cost	High	High	High
Tamper proof	Good to excellent	Excellent	Good to Excellent
Sizes	½″ & ¾″ diameter tubes up to 46″	Variety of sizes and shapes	1″ & ¾″ sq. tube, 8′-10′ long
Color/finish	Polished chrome plate or matte black	Brushed aluminum	Chrome or matte black
Remarks	If not properly designed, chrome tubes could dominate an exhibit; otherwise a very versatile system.	Somewhat fussy to assemble and disassemble; can have a "heavy" appearance; otherwise a very versatile system.	Plastic inserts for connectors have to be replaced when system is reused.

*See "Sources," page 160, for addresses and telephone numbers.
The illustrations of the various "commerical systems" only show their
salient features and are not intended to show all details and accessories.

Figure 72 System Abstracta

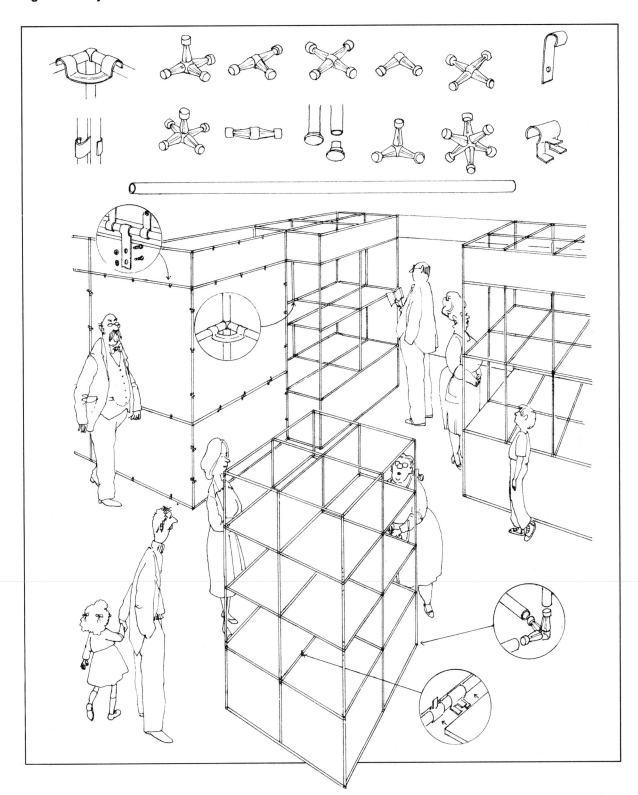

Figure 73   Alka Structures

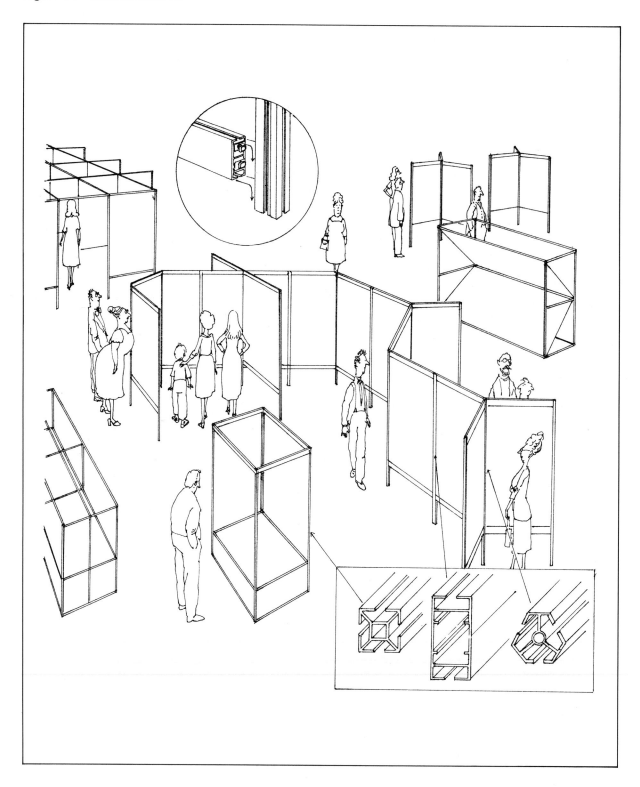

Figure 74   Apton System

System*	Bigscreen System Fig. 75	System Connectra Fig. 76	System 8 Fig. 77
Basic description	Pole and panel system	Panel "griptube" and connector system and panel framing capabilities	Tubular steel frame and panel system
Structure only	No	Yes	No
Panels only	No	No	No
Client supplies panels	No	Yes	No
Complete system	Yes	No	Yes
Can create exhibit cases	No	Yes	No
Structural versatility	Limited	Excellent	Limited
Has its own lighting system	Yes	None	Yes
Durability of parts	Excellent	Excellent	Excellent
Ease of assembly	Excellent	Good to excellent	Excellent
Ease of disassembly	Excellent	Excellent	Excellent
Strength and stability	Fair to good	Good to excellent	Fair to good
Appearance	Good	Excellent	Good
Weight of system	Light	Light to medium	Light
Compactness for storage	Excellent	Excellent	Excellent
Accessories	Limited	Limited	Limited
Cost	Medium	Low	Low
Tamper proof	Good to excellent	Excellent	Fair to good
Sizes	7' poles and varied panel sizes	Cut to your specifications	1" diameter tube, 3'6"x7' frame
Color/finish	Chromed steel poles, framed panels cloth covered, variety of colors	Chrome, nickel, stainless steel; black connectors	Chrome tube; white or black panels
Remarks	A lightweight pole and panel system; does have provisions for picture hooks	Extremely versatile system, unobtrusive. Heavy panels can be used with a ⅛" spine and connected to the system. Normally ⅛" panels or plastic are used.	Size of panels and lightness of structure are a limitation.

*See "Sources," page 160, for addresses and telephone numbers.
The illustrations of the various "commerical systems" only show their
salient features and are not intended to show all details and accessories.

Figure 75   Bigscreen System

Figure 76 System Connectra

Figure 77 System 8

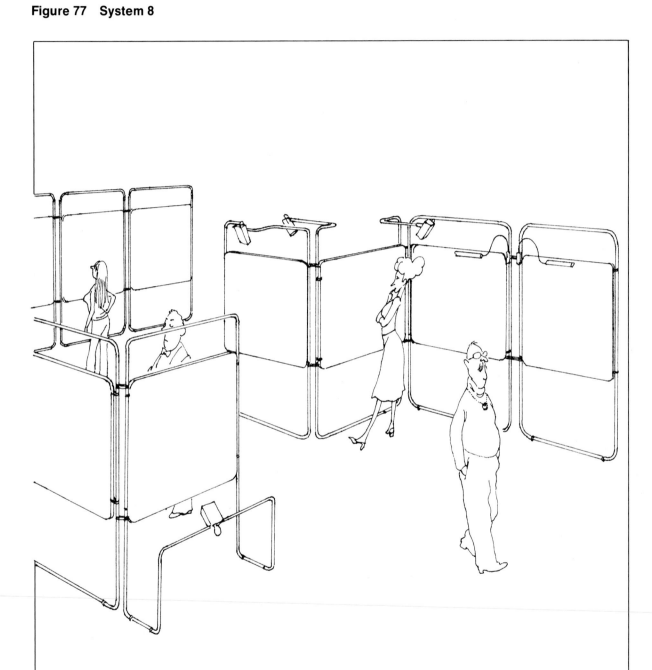

System	Gallery Panel System Fig. 78	Klem Fastener System Fig. 79	Multiscreen System Fig. 80
Basic description	Self-contained double-faced panel system	Brushed chrome jaw connector with rubber inserts in two sizes: Maxi-Klem & Mini-Klem	Modular panel system with connectors
Structure only	No	No	No
Panels only	Yes	No	Yes
Client supplies panels	No	Yes	No
Complete system	No	No	Yes
Can create exhibit cases	See remarks	Yes	Yes
Structural versatility	Limited	Excellent	Good
Has its own lighting system	Yes	None	Yes
Durability of parts	Excellent	Excellent	Excellent
Ease of assembly	Excellent	Excellent	Excellent
Ease of disassembly	Excellent	Excellent	Excellent
Strength and stability	Excellent	Excellent	Good
Appearance	Excellent	Excellent	Fair to good
Weight of system	Heavy	Light	Light
Compactness for storage	Good	Excellent	Excellent
Accessories	Limited	Limited	Varied
Cost	High	Low	Medium
Tamper proof	Excellent	Good to excellent	Good
Sizes	4'x8' panels or smaller	approximately 3" & approximately 2"	Modular sizes, varied
Color/finish	Variety of burlap & vinyl covering	Brushed chrome with black rubber inserts	Bright chrome frames, choice of panel colors
Remarks	Incorporates a continuous hanging strip along with concealed electrical service. Exhibit cases can be ordered to work with the panel system based upon the client's needs.	A versitile connector withstands extremely high tensions and pressures.	Somewhat light in weight and limited as far as mounting works of art. Works best for light graphics or photographic exhibits. Has a "busy" appearance.

Figure 78   Gallery Panel System

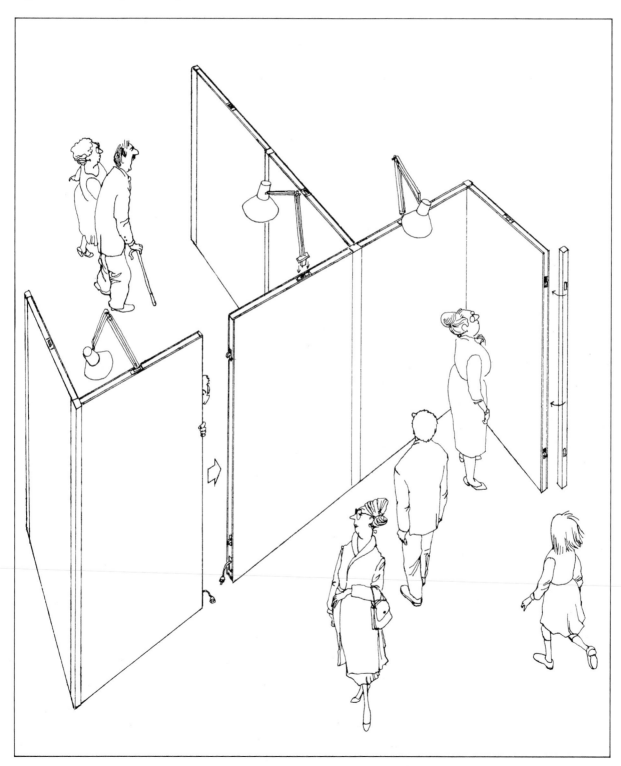

Figure 79   Klem Fastener System

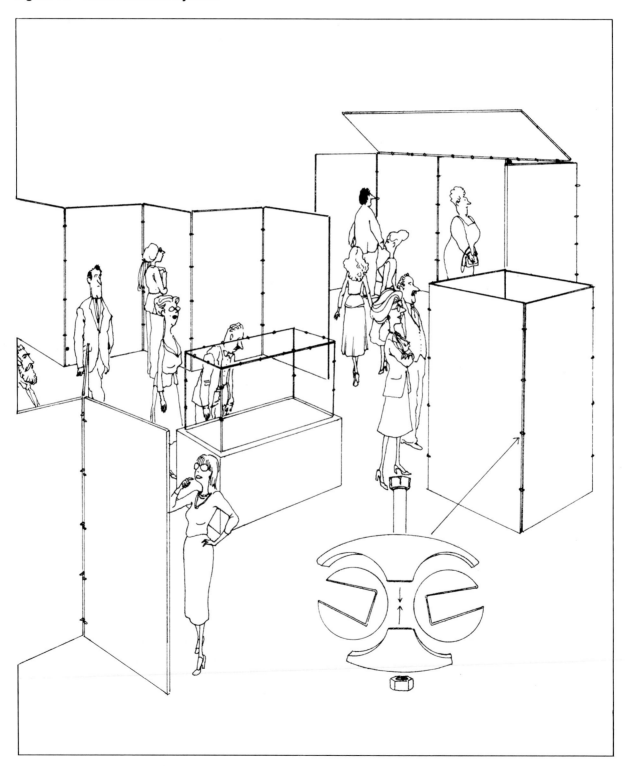

Figure 80 Multiscreen System

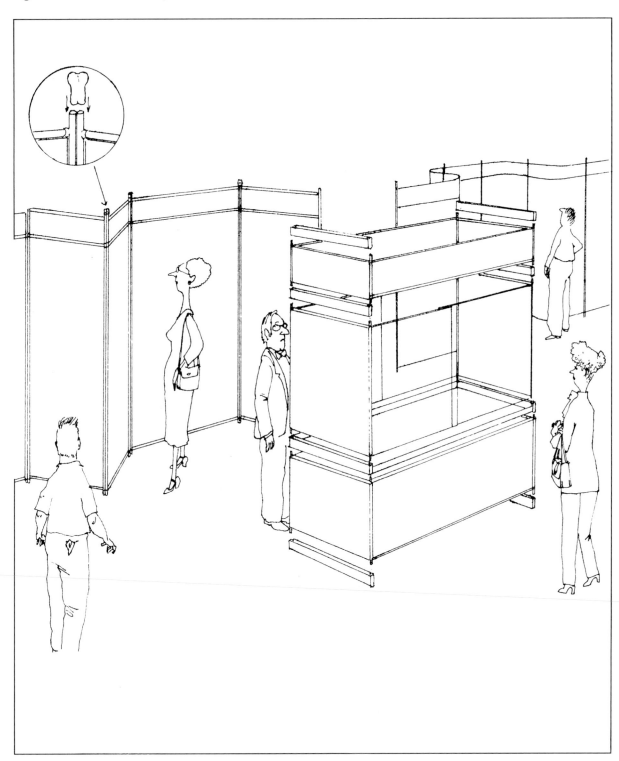

System*	Opto System Fig. 81	Sho-Wall Fig. 82	Unistrut Fig. 83
Basic description	Tubular steel system with a series of clamps	Self-contained double-faced panel system	Steel channel system of varying weights & sizes
Structure only	Yes	No	Yes
Panels only	No	Yes	No
Client supplies panels	Yes	No	Yes
Complete system	No	No	No
Can create exhibit cases	Yes	No	Yes
Structural versatility	Excellent	Limited	Excellent
Has its own lighting system	None	Yes	None
Durability of parts	Excellent	Excellent	Excellent
Ease of assembly	Good	Good	Excellent
Ease of disassembly	Excellent	Excellent	Excellent
Strength and stability	Excellent	Good to excellent	Excellent
Appearance	Excellent	Good	Good to excellent
Weight of system	Heavy	Light to medium	Very heavy
Compactness for storage	Excellent	Good	Excellent
Accessories	Extremely varied	Limited	Varied
Cost	High	Medium	Medium
Tamper proof	Excellent	Good to excellent	Excellent
Sizes	1″ diameter tubes up to 16′5″ long	From 3′ wide to 8′; height from 4′6″ to 7′	Varied according to need
Color/finish	Buff, brown or chrome clamps; brass, chrome or color PVC tubes	Wide variety of textiles and colors	Must be painted for client
Remarks	The system could dominate an exhibit if not carefully designed, very versatile.	The maximum height of 7′ for the free-standing panels is a limitation. There is a spring-loaded compression system for solid ceilings which raises the panel height.	A very sturdy steel structure with great versatility its only drawback is its weight.

*See ''Sources,'' page 160, for addresses and telephone numbers.
The illustrations of the various ''commerical systems'' only show their
salient features and are not intended to show all details and accessories.

Figure 81   Opto System

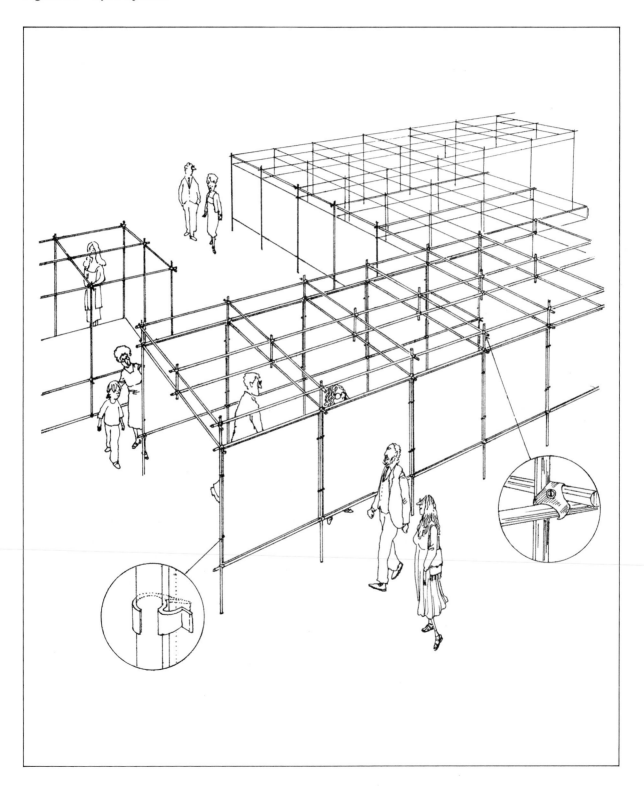

Figure 82   Sho-Wall

Figure 83   Unistrut

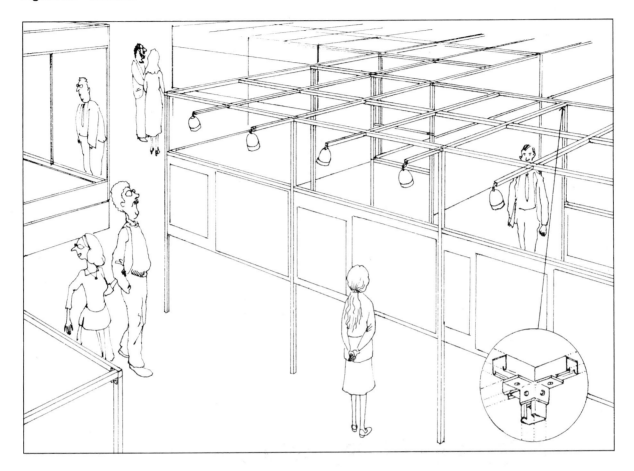

Other systems* (channels, space frames, tubes and connectors, etc.) which have exhibition potential are:

Mero Building System (space frame)
Telespar Tubing & Movable Partition System
Power-Strut Channel System
Triodetic Structures (space frame)
P.G. Structures (space frame)
Julius Blum (tubing and connectors)
Lawrence Metal (tubing, frames and connectors)

There are many additional industrial manufacturers (local and national) that produce slotted angle irons, tubing and connectors, frames as well as channel systems and can also be contacted for information. Many products manufactured for industrial use, such as light weight structures and industrial shelving, are easily and quite effectively adapted for exhibit structures. □

*See Sources, page 160, for listing of manufacturers, dealers or sales representatives.

Chapter 4

Illumination

4

Illumination

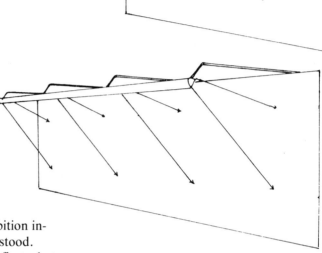

■ Lighting

Lighting is a critical element in an exhibition installation. It can also be the least understood.

When designing your show, consider first what objects you are displaying and plan to light them with the visitor's point of view in mind; then think about enclosures, cases and panels and how they should be illuminated effectively.

Artificial lighting, which can be focused, moved, intensified or dimmed, and which is totally independent of the outdoors, is the ideal. Like any other medium, it must be handled with common sense. All exhibitions require an overall illumination, so that people can find their way around comfortably. Since the eye will always focus on a brilliant spot, lighting is the easiest way to place emphasis on an object or area. By the same token, lack of it can be used to "hide" dull corners and give contrast to bright areas. An even light is desired for paintings, framed objects and textiles while for three-dimensional objects a more dramatic effect will emphasize form, solidity and surface qualities.

We suggest that anyone involved with exhibit installation read about the art and science of lighting.* Certain terms, however, may be confusing, especially when it comes to measuring light levels or illumination value. In international

Figure 84

Filament or incandescent lamps give the most efficient illumination but can dazzle the eye. They must therefore be placed out of the line of sight and in a location so the light beam does not reflect into the viewers' eyes. Light bounces off a surface at the same angle at which it hits that surface.

Figure 85

To illuminate a wall surface evenly, the light source should never be closer than the proportion of one to four, otherwise "hot spots" on the wall surface will be noticeable while leaving the bottom of the panel in relative darkness.

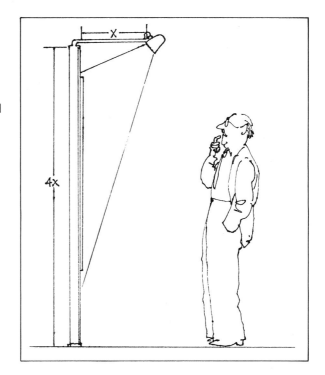

journals and publications, illumination is measured in *lux* where 1 lux equals 1 lumen per square meter. In Great Britain and in the United States illumination is still quoted lumens per square foot or footcandles. One lumen per square foot equals approximately 10 lux.

There are two main types of artificial illumination, fluorescent and filament or incandescent lamps. Fluorescent lamps provide an even, shadowless emission of light; they are extremely economical and come in cold or warm colors. However, they cannot be focused and do not project parallel beams of light. They are best used to provide general illumination, or next to a flat white surface that reflects light from the back of the tube. Its major drawback is the considerable amount of ultraviolet radiation it emits that is extremely harmful to pigments, paper and organic materials such as wool, fur and feathers. If there are fluorescent lamps in your facility, cover the tubes with U-V filter sleeves or use Verilux (a trade name) tubes to eliminate much of the radiation.

Filament lamps, on the other hand, have an insignificant ultraviolet emission, but produce considerable heat (which is also harmful if the lamp source is too close to the object being illuminated). They are more expensive to burn, though there are some low voltage lamps available that reduce the cost. Filament lamps offer more flexibility, particularly for special lighting effects.

A variety of filament lamps is available, each

*Prime source: "Lighting of Art Galleries and Museums," Illuminating Engineering Society, Technical Report No. 14, London, 1970. Additional sources, see Bibliography p.166.

designed for a particular purpose. Flood lamps give a general light in one direction. Spot lamps and parallel beam reflectors throw a light beam at a considerable distance with sharp shadows. A focused spot lamp (with a lens system incorporated into the light fixture) can throw a beam of considerable length, focused sharply on an object. For light to travel farther, higher wattage is required; for example, two 100-watt lamps give off the same light as one 200-watt lamp, although the one 200-watt lamp will throw the light further.

Some things to remember: fluorescent lamps behind a translucent ceiling give off an even flood of top light (shadows are almost non-existent); indirect light reflected from a ceiling produces a pleasant soft light, but is insufficient to illuminate exhibits; spot lights from a ceiling can highlight exhibits dramatically, but will not give adequate general lighting; lamps should be arranged to give direct light on exhibits and general light for the overall space.

If you have a fixed lighting system that allows for no flexibility, you may have to supplement it with lights mounted on panels (clamp-on flood or spot light or even fluorescent) or on freestanding units if the ceiling is high enough. It might be necessary to place lights near the floor to create an "up light" much like theatrical footlights.

If the ceiling has standard recessed fluorescent tubes, you might paint the ceiling dark and install louvers on the fixtures to diminish reflections;

then place cases directly beneath the fixtures. If the cases are table-top or desk-type with a shallow angle of glass, a neutral tone panel hung above it may be effective. Illuminate the panel so that the light falls onto the case. Line the case interior in a neutral shade.

To arrange the lighting before the objects are in place, assemble the following items: ladder or

Figure 86

The effect of modeling is achieved by the direction and dominant angle of the light flow.

Highly diffused light tends to flatten shape and form, suppress detail and dull the sheen or glaze of metals, ceramics and many embroidered or woven

fabrics. On the other hand, excessively sharp, direct lighting can give an unduly harsh appearance.

mechanical lift, and a selection of lamp fixtures and bulbs, spots and floods in a number of wattages.

Ideally, a gallery in which temporary exhibits are continually shown should have flexible modular lighting capabilities. This means a track-lighting system that will offer all the flexibility you need. A manufacturer or an agent for a track-lighting company will give you a cost estimate to install a system in your gallery.

If you already have track lights or fixed lighting, you may still want some outside advice. Persons involved with theatrical lighting (a theater group, high school or college drama department) may be willing to give assistance. Also, a photographer knowledgeable in studio lighting may help, or a store's display staff, which usually has someone on board who understands lighting.

■ Lighting for Emphasis and Modeling

If items are to be viewed to their best advantage, they must be lighted so that their special features are brought out most effectively. The eye is always drawn to the brightest and most strongly accented parts of a scene. Lighting, therefore, should highlight the objects without being overdone. Sometimes a strong punch of light on an object in a dark surrounding, or against a powerful contrasting background color, may rivet attention, but it can at the same time prevent details from being seen clearly. Some general illumination in addition to localized lighting is almost always desirable.

The modeling effect of light is often needed to reveal the true shape and texture of objects. (Figure 86). Study each object to see what traits to emphasize.

Some idea of lighting can be roughed out in advance when you work on the full-scale mock-ups of cases and scale model of the gallery. As mentioned earlier, a reflected ceiling plan is absolutely necessary to locate the lighting fixtures in relation to panels and cases, and indicate spot or flood lights and wattages.

After everything is in place and you "fine-tune" the lighting, you may still have to experiment a little on site. Your needs may sometimes conflict, so watch out for glare and reflections as well as emphasis and modeling.

■ Color of Light and Background

Visual adaptation operates with respect to the color of light and to light intensity or brightness. This means that daylight reflected into your

Objects and Light	Recommended Maximum Value of Illumination*
Objects insensitive to light, e.g. metal, stone, glass, ceramics, stained glass, jewelry and enamel	Unlimited, but in practice subject to display and radiant heat considerations
Oil and tempera painting, undyed leather, horn, ivory, wood, and lacquer (oriental & European)	150 lux or 15 footcandles
Objects specially sensitive to light, e.g. textiles, costumes, watercolors, tapestries, prints and drawings, stamps, manuscripts, miniatures, paintings in distemper media, call papers, gouache, dyed leather and many natural history exhibits, especially those including skins, insects and botanical specimens.	50 lux or 5 footcandles

exhibit area, color of walls, floor panels (or any colored or non-colored surface from which light can bounce) will have an overall effect on how visitors perceive the exhibit.

Colors are either warm or cool. Tungsten filament lamps are warm with exaggeration at the red end of the color spectrum; thus reds and oranges appear emphasized in comparison with their appearance in daylight. Though they are warm and cool, most fluorescent lamps are intrinsically strong in the green, blue and yellow regions. The effect of different light sources on the colors of objects is called "color rendering." In practice, *cool* fluorescent lamps are compared with *cool* daylight, while *warm* fluorescent lamps are compared with *warm* incandescent sources that are realized by tungsten filament lamps. The choice in practice between different types of fluorescent lamps should be made in terms both of color rendering and of color appearance—that is, warm versus cool. Good color rendering is always desirable but is particularly significant at exhibits that stress the importance of color, as in the case of paintings and textiles.

The background color of a wall or panel has a tremendous influence on the effectiveness of the exhibition. It should give the illusion of being recessed in relation to the display. This does not exclude the use of a vivid background, provided that illumination is focused on the object(s). If the display arrangement makes it difficult to achieve a gradation of illumination, then select a weaker background shade. Avoid bright patterns since they can detract from the object. If you are creating an environmental context as one of your exhibit's educational objectives, however, these rules do not hold true.

When a very light background is used for the display of dark objects, they should have a small and darker background of their own. Details in the dark objects can be lost unless there is a separation of intermediate tone to assist viewing. The reverse is also true; that is, for very light objects displayed against a dark background.

A white or off-white matte surface is one most often used as a background for modern paintings. This, however, creates a sharp contrast between

the paintings and the background that can actually be a detriment. For better viewing, the background color should be in a light tone of neutral value like beige, buff or light warm gray, avoiding excessive contrast. Try it in one of your installations and see if it doesn't work.

A consideration when lighting wall-mounted cases or cases mounted on a large display panel is that a reflection of himself and his surroundings on the glass may interfere with the visitor's vision. To avoid this, place the light source almost

Figure 87

A row of UV-filtered fluorescent tubes can also be used to "wall wash" and to illuminate flat elements on a wall or panel.

overhead but slightly in front of the perpendicular glass case front. If the light source were located further from the wall, the viewer would stand between the light source and the object, casting a shadow on the display.

Generally a row of 40-watt fluorescent lamps (with UV filters) or equally spaced flood lamps are best to give a soft, overall illumination to wall-hung panels. Key elements mounted on the panels or on the wall can be highlighted with individual directional spotlights or even a lens-type spotlight fitted with a mask that can shape the beam to the object being illuminated. Be sure the light source is not located so that the viewer passing in front of its beam will create a shadow.

■ How Much Light to Use?

Tapestries, carpets and rare textiles should be given a low value of illumination with UV filtration, since too much light will deteriorate them.

Costumes present a serious conservation problem. Consequently, the illuminations should be low, and UV filters used. Choose lamps that provide color rendering appropriate to the display. Tungsten filament lamps add a touch of sparkle and modeling.

When displaying **glass,** many techniques are possible. Spotlighting cut glass will emphasize facets that are often best seen against a dark background. Translucent glass may need some front light to show modeling and decoration. Opaque glass should be treated as ceramic, with strong front or side light for modeling against a slightly rough, neutral background. Take care to avoid mirror images of the light sources in the glaze.

Weapons, armor and large metal objects work well with general lighting supplemented by spotlights to pick up luster and modeling. Metal objects of a silvery or steel cast will frequently be enhanced by a pale blue or gray background. Gold, on the other hand, looks best against a dark, rich, velvety background.

General lighting is usually satisfactory for **furniture** displayed alone or in small groupings. If the view is limited, as in part of a room or enclosure, shop window lighting techniques are suitable (an overhead light source is directed at the objects). Conservation is an important consideration, especially if fabrics and textiles are combined with furniture. In this case, place incandescent lamps at a distance so that their heat will not reach the textiles. Use UV filters along with fluorescent lamps.

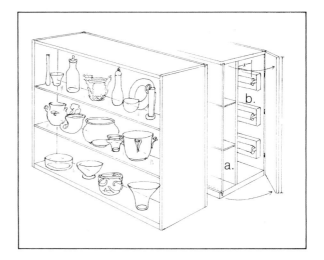

Figure 88 Glassware Lighting

Transparent and translucent glass is shown to best advantage on glass shelves against a softly illuminated background, perhaps a luminous panel (a). Inside the lightbox, painted in matte white, are three fluorescent tubes (b).

Books, manuscripts and stamps are usually displayed in cases. As conservation is a problem, use UV filters and limit the illumination to the appropriate level, not exceeding 5 footcandles.

Coins, medals and seals are also displayed in cases. Some directional lighting will help to accentuate the relief of the objects. To assist the perception of fine detail, a dark background should be used, but the brightness contrast between object and background should not be too great.

Jewelry and fine metal are best shown off with tungsten filament lamps, especially where cut stones are displayed. Avoid excessive temperature rise within the exhibit case. If fluorescent lamps are used, they should be a warm color for gold and brass and an intermediate color for silver and steel. Small pieces of jewelry are usually best displayed against a dark matte background.

Sculpture of stone, metal, clay, plaster and wood is usually not harmed by light except for painted wood. Some directional lighting looks good on sculpture-in-the-round—adding spotlights will help. Use light ''modeling'' on sculpture, with most of it coming from one side and not from behind the viewer. Avoid direct frontal lighting.

Very shallow carved panels are best lighted by means of fluorescent lamps located slightly above them. Carving in high relief requires light at a less acute angle; a combination of tungsten filament and fluorescent lamps will enhance modeling and texture.

Heat from incandescent lights can be damaging to ivory and bone, therefore the lamps should be kept out of the case if possible. If not, a low voltage incandescent lamp connected to a rheostat is recommended to allow a minimum of heat build-up within the case. Another solution is to drill small holes in the case (out of sight) and plug with cotton. This will allow heat to escape but prevent dust from entering.

Some ancient religious sculptures once placed on altars were originally illuminated from below by votive candles or oil lamps. Check with your lenders to see if they were used in this manner. If so, plan for low voltage. □

Chapter 5

Titles and Labels

5

Titles and Labels

■ Titles and Labels

After the initial visual impression of an exhibition, successful communication depends upon the integration of the elements—objects or specimens, photographs, maps, reconstructions, models. The story line is communicated through titles, subheadings and labels that should be in harmony with the total design concept.

The title is a short statement of the subject, such as "Polish Posters" or "Buildings Reborn: New Uses, Old Places." Labels vary in length and provide identification as well as explanation. They are placed next to the object.

A traveling exhibition always comes complete with label copy, area headings and title panel. If you include your own objects, you will need to add labels in the same style. Their preparation includes writing, design, production and installation.

■ Writing Copy

Labels integrate the exhibition as well as identify objects. Together the display and text work to tell a story. An outline, or script, with factual information about the exhibit's objects and concept will ultimately be abstracted for label copy.

Labels should be brief and to the point. It is always tempting to slip in extra detail in the belief that someone will find it interesting. Generally, additional words and a large chunk of text tend to discourage people before they even start to read.

Although exhibitions are usually aimed at attracting the general public, you must select an audience for the text. We generally recommend that you write for the 15-year-old education level (newspaper English is geared to the 12- to 13-year-old). However, you should evaluate each exhibition for its particular audience and adapt the text accordingly.

Attempts have been made to increase comprehension by supplementing labels with a fact sheet or booklet for the visitor to keep. Some institutions have handed out bibliographies for different education levels—primary and secondary school, and adult. Another option is to provide guided lectures, although this, of course, limits the visitor who likes to explore for himself. For large exhibits, some museums use an electronic "audio-tour," which can accommodate several education levels and foreign languages.

A label writing check list:

1.   Is the story line of the exhibit accurately and concisely formulated?

2.   Does the text reflect the vocabulary and assumed knowledge of the target audience?

3.   Are labels worded with a view to clarity rather than to verbal economy?

4.   Are labels overloaded with information? (There should be no more than five to seven items of information per general label.)

5.   Are there any superfluous labels?

6.   Have the following rules-of-thumb been taken into account?

a.   Keep sentences short: 10 to 15 words where possible, never more than 22.

b.   Limit subordinate clauses to one or two at the most.

c.   Try not to invert sentences (i.e., do put main clause first).

d.   Try to keep the natural word order.

e.   Avoid ambiguity.

f.   Use a full stop (period) rather than a comma where possible.

g.   Don't worry about repeating nouns if they are the best descriptive terms.

h.   Avoid passive tense where possible.

i.   Use short paragraphs (two or three sentences is not too short).

j.   Always explain unfamiliar words and concepts as soon as they appear.

k.   Relate events and dates, if the exhibition covers another culture or time period, to dates and events familiar to the viewer.

7.   Do the labels and the display materials tell the story?

Assuming that the interest of the most casual visitor has been aroused by the title and the eye-catching elements of the exhibit, give him a short, simple statement in the introductory label or text. It should encourage him to seek further information. Somewhere in the gallery provide a brief bibliography of popular and scholarly publications for those interested.

■ Typography and Readability

If you prepare your own labels, you should have some knowledge of typography and printing. (For further reading, see bibliography on page 166.) The title is most important, so choose a contrasting typeface, larger size and different color for emphasis. Cutout or three-dimensional letters work well for the main title and can be used in a smaller size for subheadings. The use of all capital letters is permissible in short statements and titles, but not advisable for longer labels. Because our eyes have become accustomed to the lower-case letters of books and newsprint, they should be used so the viewer can read with speed and accuracy. You may or may not find it necessary

to adopt special techniques to make exhibition typography look interesting, but you must always make a definite choice of letters to be used. The few standard typefaces in current use were all initially designed for body matter in books or newsprint. When you have chosen a typeface as the most suitable for a particular job, use it consistently. Different kinds of typefaces appearing throughout a display are not only distracting but are the hallmark of amateur typography.

The main introductory label should be designed to catch the eye at the entrance of the exhibit. The general label for an area or a case should never be placed close to an object but in a location prominent and high enough for several persons to read simultaneously. A 72-point type (about ¾″ high for a capital letter) is a minimum size for the general label. Secondary labels should be placed next to the objects they describe.

One of the requisites for legibility is consistency; others are design of typeface, type size, length of line and spacing of lines. Visibility refers to the capacity of being seen or distinguished against a background. Legibility is not possible without high visibility, but high visibility does not guarantee high legibility.

Three factors determine good visibility and readability: illumination, size and contrast. For illumination, an absolute minimum of five foot-candles should be used (measured on the object or label shown). Size of the typeface for secondary labels (object labels) should be no smaller than 24 point and, if space permits, even 30 point. Contrast between the letters and the background should be as strong as possible; black letters on a white background are best. Although equally strong, light-color letters on a dark background color should be the same color as the wall or case. For the best results, a sample label should be tested for readability under lighting conditions similar to those planned for the exhibit. Regardless of the background color, increasing the size of the typeface will result in better legibility.

If you have an "island case," one in which an object can be viewed from all four sides, place a label on each side so that several visitors can read at the same time.

18 pt. Garamond, roman ——————

16 pt. Garamond, italic and roman ———

12 pt. Garamond, italic ———————

Raymond Steth

Evolution of Swing, WPA/FAP 1935–42
Lithograph

*Lent by the Howard University Gallery of Art,
Washington, D.C.*

BEACH SOLITUDE

Pieced

Florida   Ann Humphries

"Creating a new and 'only mine' quilt is my first love. . . . What more reward could one need than to see their idea come alive?" Ann Humphries has been quilting for almost 30 years. Her quilt symbolizes south Florida's beaches, water, and sun.

——— 18 pt. Garamond Bold, all caps

——— 11 pt. Century Schoolbook, italic

——— 11 pt. Century Schoolbook, roman

– 16 pt./18 Century Schoolbook, roman

Figure 89   These sample exhibit labels show simple, readable, yet effective uses of typography

■ Lettering and Reproduction

Three-dimensional letters are good for short titles and subtitles, and the added dimension helps to give the title emphasis. These letters are available in many sizes and materials—cardboard, cork, plaster, metal, plastic and wood. Catalogs showing the range of typefaces and sizes may be obtained at art supply stores. If ready-made letters are too expensive, you can cut letters by hand in most of the above materials with a coping saw or jigsaw. A master set of letters can also be cut out and additional castings made using a latex mold.

Lettering for titles and subtitles should be done by a professional, but this can be expensive. Poor hand lettering reveals the amateur and always results in inferior readability. If your budget is tight, use a Leroy lettering guide; but understand that you will have to practice a long time before the results are even passable.

The amateur, with some practice and a good sense of letter spacing, can also make fairly adequate titles by using pressure-sensitive wax letters (Lettraset Press Type, etc.) These commercially printed alphabets are available in almost all typefaces and sizes, and can be obtained from art supply stores. Titles and subtitles can be prepared on a sheet of illustration board, then photostated to the desired size, using either the positive or negative print. The photostat can be dry or wet-mounted.

Typewriters should not be overlooked when you need to make inexpensive labels. An enlarged photostat of a typewritten label can be mounted on a card or a piece of hardboard. Bulletin (large type) and electric models with changeable typefaces are useful for this purpose.

The best procedure, however, for making letters is to have them set in type. These can also be photostated in the same size or enlarged, no more than three times, since irregularities may show up in greater enlargements. A typesetter or printer will supply information on the styles available. The printer or typesetter may even be willing to donate his or her services, with proper credit, of course, in the exhibit. You might also contact a high school or trade school print shop for free assistance.

An exhibition with many elements of design (objects, artwork, photographs, reconstructions, maps, charts and labels) will look less cluttered, and therefore more pleasing to the eye, by eliminating separate, contrasting labels printed on cards. One way of doing this is to print labels on brown kraft paper that has been painted, by brush or roller or even spray gun, the same color as the background of your panel or case interior. The only disadvantage, and it is a slight one, is that the edge of the paper is still visible, and one is still conscious of the outline of the rectangle, however softened. Photo enlargements can be made with all the label material combined on one sheet and then mounted on the background on which to mount your objects for display.

The most professional looking labels are made with the silk-screen process. They blend into the background rather than intrude on the design. Only the typography shows. This technique also offers many color possibilities. Silk screen is more expensive because of the labor and equipment involved, but the result is more than worth the expense. The process can also be used to reproduce art work such as graphs, maps, line drawings, and even halftones in one or many colors on opaque, translucent or even transparent surfaces.

■ Dry and Wet Mounting

Labels, graphs, charts, some art work and photographs can be mounted with photographic dry mounting tissue that is heat and pressure sensitive adhesive. However, this should never be undertaken without the owner's permission; remember that the process is irreversible. It is done with a dry mounting heat press (most photo labs have them) or by using an ordinary household electric iron. A sheet of kraft paper placed on top of the material to be mounted will prevent damage.

Practice on some sample pieces before you start on the items (to avoid any damage to them). Test to make sure the elements mounted do not peel apart; if they do, use more heat and pressure. You can dry mount on illustration board,

72 pt. Garamond Bold, roman

ABCDEFGHIJ
KLMNOPQRS
TUVWXYZ ab
cdefghijklmno
pqrstuvwxyz $12

24 pt. Times Roman Bold, roman and italic

ABCDEFGHIJKLMNOPQRSTUVWXYZ
abcdefghijklmnopqrstuvwxyz .,-:;"!?()
1234567890$&

ABCDEFGHIJKLMNOPQRSTUVWXYZ
abcdefghijklmnopqrstuvwxyz
1234567890$& .,-:;"!?()

Figure 90   These full-size examples of 24 pt., 30 pt., and 72 pt. type sizes may help you determine the appropriate selection for your labels and text panels.

---

30 pt. Helvetica Medium, roman and italic

ABCDEFGHIJKLMNOPQRSTUV WXYZ abcdefghijklmnopqrstuv wxyz $1234567890& .,-:;'!?

ABCDEFGHIJKLMNOPQRSTUV WXYZ abcdefghijklmnopqrstuv wxyz $1234567890& .,-:;'!?

---

single or double ply; on Upsom board and hardboard. After the board has cooled, test for peeling and, if it is present, apply additional heat and pressure. Trim the material with a mat knife or a jigsaw.

For dry mounting color photographs, use a low temperature mounting tissue, otherwise the print may shrink.

Materials that lend themselves to wet mounting are photostats, photographs and photomurals; that is, only photographic papers. In this process, which does require considerable expertise since it is also irreversible, the photo is soaked thoroughly in a tank or large sink, laid out on a piece of glass larger than the paper, cleared of excess water with a darkroom rubber squeegee and sponge; and then placed on a piece of hardboard that has been brushed with a thin but even coat of white glue or vinyl wallpaper paste. The paper is positioned and carefully smoothed out with the squeegee. Finally, it is washed off with a clean sponge. Excess glue will be squeezed out.

Panels to be mounted should be precut to size. The mounted paper can be trimmed flush by using a razor blade or it can be wrapped around the panel onto the back. Counter-mount the hardboard panel with kraft paper or with paper of similar weight to that on the front. Countermounting will prevent the panel from buckling; when paper dries, it has tremendous pulling strength and can easily warp a ½″ hardboard panel. □

Chapter 6

Installation

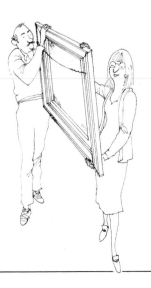

6

Installation

■ Installation

As the opening date is fixed, the installation work will have to be fitted into a very short time period. The time may even be shorter if the show is preceded by another exhibition that has to be dismantled, removed from the area, packed and shipped. It is therefore essential that you plan very carefully to insure a relatively smooth installation of the new exhibition and be prepared for unforeseen and unexpected events and problems.

The following is a sample schedule to adapt for your own use, adding or eliminating tasks depending upon the particular makeup of an exhibit. When preparing your schedule, work backward from the opening date, particularly for the "time" and "due" dates of certain tasks. Assign tasks to specific persons. If you depend upon volunteers, have some extra names to call during this critical period. One person should assume responsibility of coordinating the entire process—keeping records, assigning tasks, checking off completed tasks and keeping an eye on the time.

■ General Preparation

When the area is emptied and closed off to the public with barriers, it should be cleaned. If you are using supplemental lighting fixtures, install them now. Fill, sand and paint all cracks and holes in the walls, if necessary. If your design requires a special color scheme, paint the entire area, and remember to use a drop cloth to protect the floor.

After painting, turn your attention to lighting. If there is a flexible track system, set it according to the scale plan drawings. If the lighting is fixed and you need supplemental fixtures, these should be installed before you paint, as mentioned above. If you plan to mount lights on panels and structures, paint first and install the fixtures after panels and structures are in place.

When the painting and light arranging is finished, you may need to clean the area again. Now move in a couple of work tables, tools and supplies for the installation.

■ Wall-Hung Exhibitions

If the exhibition includes both wall-hung and freestanding elements, install the important wall-hung ones first to clear the area of materials and clutter. The center of your space will be ready for the freestanding elements.

Check panels and cases for final adjustments. Does the glass fit properly? If not, trim the glass or trim the wood, whichever is easier. If you are using case inserts, either plain or cloth-wrapped, make sure they fit, too. You may have to do a little trimming but don't wait until the case is installed in the gallery. Make sure also that each panel and case is identified by a code number corresponding to the number used in your scale plan drawing and placed out-of-sight. This will aid in moving elements into their locations.

□ *Mounting Labels and Objects*
Labels, art work and photographs on hardboard are mounted on panels in several ways: toeing-in (nailing in small brads or pins at an angle at the edge of the label panels, and then snipping off the brad), gluing, using double-faced foam tape, or screwing. (The latter is least desirable because the screw heads are obvious.) Always use a level to make sure the labels are parallel to the top and bottom of the panel.

Exhibit Preparation and Installation Schedule

*Exhibit Title:*_____   *Opening Date:*_____

Tasks	*Name of Assigned Person*	*Time & Due Dates*
1. Planning: develop research & exhibit script (if an in-house project) and prepare project budget; develop object, painting or specimen list		
2. Design: prepare scale model & scale drawings		
3. Assemble support materials (photos, etc.)		
4. Label copy: preliminary		
5. Purchase fabrication materials & supplies		
6. Fabricate exhibit elements & mounting devices		
7. Prepare maps, charts, reconstructions, etc.		
8. Finalize label copy		
9. Produce graphics (labels, title panels, maps, etc.)		
10. Clear exhibit area of previous exhibition & clean area; close it to public		
11. Paint exhibit area (if necessary)		
12. Unpack traveling exhibit or assemble your own objects in one central, secure area		
13. Set lighting in preliminary locations in exhibit area		
14. Paint panels, exhibit cases & case furniture		
15. Affix graphics to panels		
16. Move work tables into exhibit area		
17. Move wall-hung panels & other wall-mounted elements into exhibit area along with hardware & supplies		
18. Move tools or tool cart into exhibit area along with hardware & supplies		
19. Install wall-mounted elements		
20. Move free-standing exhibit elements and/or structure into exhibit area		
21. Assemble free-standing elements or structure		
22. Move exhibit cases into area & attach where necessary		
23. Bring exhibit case furniture into area and install; also object mounts, cradles, etc., and install; clean area		
24. Affix all remaining labels		
25. Move objects into area & install		
26. Photograph cases with objects		
27. Clean case interiors & install glass		
28. Touch-up		
29. Set final lighting		
30. Clean area		
31. Arrange plants		

If you are using three-dimensional letters for headings, paint and glue them to panels away from the exhibition area. Here is a recommended method of painting: Attach lengths of masking tape sticky side up on a scrap piece of cardboard with a bit of tape at either end. Press the letters on the tape. Paint them with either a brush, spray gun or spray can.

For equal spacing, cut long strips of brown wrapping paper about two inches wide, making sure the edges are straight. Tape the "ribbon" of paper to a scrap panel and lay out the three-dimensional letters along the top edge of the ribbon. Space them so the words are easily readable—not too tight and not too much space. With a pencil, mark the beginning and end of each let-

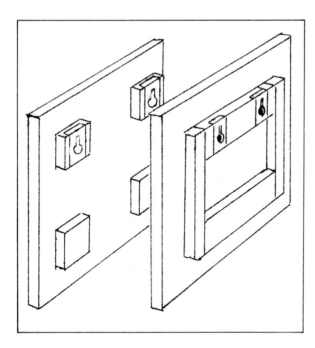

Figure 91   "Floating" Panel

A small, wall-hung panel can be made by attaching glue blocks with keyhole plates to the back. The panel is secured by placing it over the screw head and moving it downward.

ter on the paper ribbon below, also writing the name of the letter. The letters, O, S, C, Q, G, and U can be indicated through their center lines. Some letters descend below the ordinary horizontal line of the letters, including lower case s, y, g, o, q, p, j; and in some type designs the letter a and x and upper case letters Q, O, and S. If you do not allow for this in laying out the letters, they will look irregular or "bouncy." There is no surer sign of amateurism than poorly spaced or uneven typography in exhibit headings.

When the paper ribbons are marked and letters painted, you are ready to attach them to the panels. Tack the paper ribbon in place on the panel with little strips of masking tape, making sure the top edge of ribbon is level. A yardstick will not work because of the "descenders." Now apply a thin coat of white glue to the back of the letters and press them to the panel. If large letters begin to slip, tape them lightly with slivers of masking tape, removing them after an hour. For descending letters, glue only the part above the horizontal line. Attach large letters with descenders after all the other letters are glued and paper ribbon removed. You will have to glue these in place "by eye." Or if you have some misgivings about this, cut a notch in the paper ribbon to accommodate each descender.

Some three-dimensional objects can be mounted directly onto panels with plastic coated wire (Figure 92). Check first with the lender to see if this is permitted.

Surface-mounted objects can be protected by attaching a plastic sheet two or three inches away from the panel (Figure 93). This attachment can be made only before the display panel is installed in the gallery, since the "securing" is done on the reverse side. This is also the time to anchor hanging exhibit cases to large panels. Bolt the case to the panel with interior panels and glass removed.

□ *Hanging Devices*

With your display panels painted, connecting devices attached, labels and non-breakable objects fastened and exhibit area prepared, you are now ready to install hanging devices. Picture rods, braided wire and drilling were discussed on page 46, so by this time you know what best suits your circumstances. Guided by the scale plan drawing, measure and mark with tape the exact location of each wall-hung element. Move picture rods or wire to the right spot, drill holes and insert fasteners. Then carefully move display panels into the gallery. Regardless of the amount

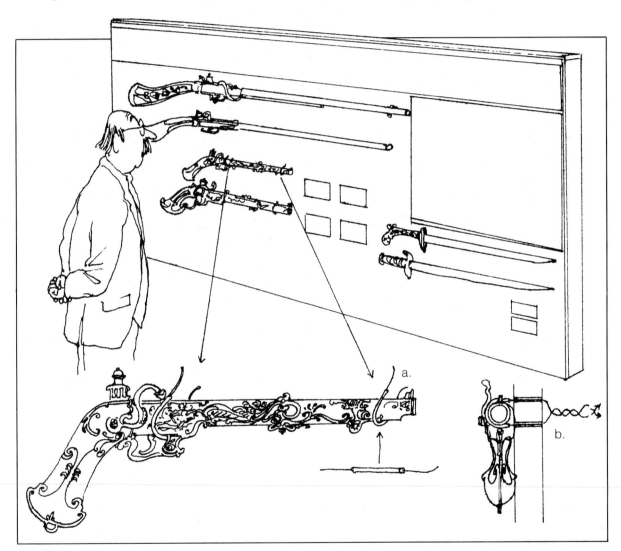

Figure 92   Wired Objects

Many objects like weapons or chunks of rock can be wired. Locate at least two points of support, hold the object up against the panel and mark the points where the wire will pass through. Drill four small holes just large enough for the wire. Use fine plastic-coated copper wire or steel wire sheathed in plastic tubing that has a high tensile strength. Pass it around the object and through the holes (a). An aide should be ready on the other side to grip the loose ends and twist them together (b). Sometimes an additional small cloth or felt pad is necessary to prevent the coated wire from biting into the object.

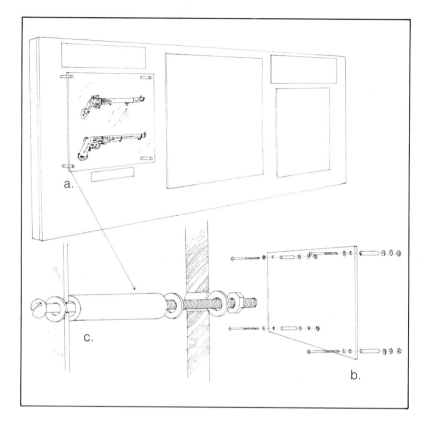

Figure 93   Plastic Cover

A protective sheet of ¼″ plastic is bolted at four corners and held out from the display panel with metal or wooden posts (a). Drill four holes into both the panel and plastic. Using bolts, four post pieces, washers and nuts attach the sheet (b). The cross-section view (c) shows hardware inserted through the plastic, left, and the panel, right. In the center is the post with washers at either side. At left is a bolt and at right a nut.

Figure 94   "Holding Jig"

A piece of lumber nailed to a couple of sawhorses becomes a "holding jig" on which to rest a panel at the right location for hanging. This support will also hold the panel level.

of help on hand, bring in only one panel at a time. Some workers can hang panels while others prepare hanging devices. Use a "holding jig" if several panels are to be installed at the same height, particularly if done with picture rods or wire (Figure 94). Wear cotton gloves to handle panels finished with flat paint, and have a carpenter's level handy to make sure everything is straight.

□ Textiles and Costumes

Many means have been devised for displaying textiles and, fortunately, fabrics are fairly adaptable to different forms of presentation. Large pieces—rugs, quilts, wall hangings and table linens—may be mounted on long poles or boards that can be suspended from the ceiling or walls by means of picture wire (Figure 95). Display textiles should *never* be nailed, tacked or stapled. Fragile, rare and unique pieces should be treated like paintings and mounted under glass or Plexiglas.

Figure 95   Mounting Textiles

Valuable textiles can be framed or mounted on poles or wooden strips. One method (a) is to hand-sew a Velcro tape strip using a hem stitch along the top back of the textile and then staple an identical length on the wooden batten, to which two or three screw eyes have been fastened (depending upon the weight of the textile). Press the two Velcro strips together forming a bond and install with braided picture wire. Smaller pieces of textiles may be similarly fixed to dowels or thin wooden battens attached to both top and bottom edges to hold the fabric flat. If both sides of a fabric are to be shown (b), the piece may be mounted between two wooden battens by sewing Velcro to both sides of the textile,

using the same stitch and stapling Velcro tape on the inside of the wooden battens, then pressing the two battens together. The battens should extend a few inches beyond the textile on each side, just enough to pass through a bolt. A loop of braided picture wire, pre-cut to the proper length, is placed around the bolt. Then the second batten is pressed in place and a nut screwed into the threaded bolt, holding the textile and the wire in place. In method (c), loops of tape are sewn at close intervals on the back of the textile through which the wood piece may be slipped. The end loops may have to be tacked to the wooden pole to prevent them from slipping and causing the exhibited textile to look like a shower curtain. Needless to say, all sewing should only be done with permission of the lender.

Figure 96   Costume Display

To avoid a too contemporary look of mannequins, the Costume Institute of the Metropolitan Museum of Art in New York pulls different colored nylon hose over the head to the base of the neck, tying a knot at the top and cutting off the remainder (a). Simple figure outlines made of ¾″ plywood and painted skin color are effective for displaying a costume (b). A mannequin head of plywood and paint can be used for hats and headdresses (c). A simply-cut costume like the Japanese kimono can be hung on a wooden pole suspended by wires (d).

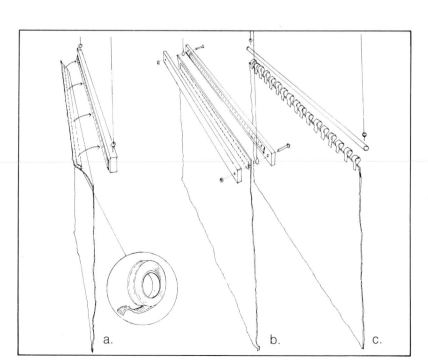

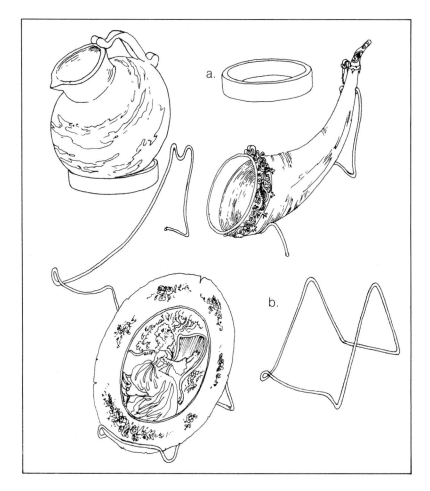

Figure 97   Cradles and Mounts

Objects with uneven bottoms or ones that may be "tippy" can rest on tubes (a). Tubes can be made of cardboard, aluminum, Plexiglas and even terra cotta drainpipe. They can be cut to hold any size object. Other devices serving as mounts are bent wire plateholders or armatures of polished metal or sprayed with Krylon lacquer (b).

Figure 98   Preparing the Objects

Finally, bring into the exhibit area the fragile objects and place them on a padded work table. Clean the valuables and the case interior with a fine animal hair brush. Wearing white cotton gloves, place the objects in position. (Greasy or perspiring fingers can dull porcelain, highly polished wood finishes, silver and other metals.)

Costumes are best shown in a manner similar to how they are worn (Figure 96). Mannequins borrowed from a department store are excellent, except that their heads have a too contemporary look that often is incompatible with ethnographic or historic costumes.

□ *Fragile Objects*
When the large display panels have been securely mounted, you are ready to install the more fragile objects. First, complete the exhibit cases, if there are any mounted on the large display panels, by installing case inserts (plain or cloth-covered panels) as gently as possible. Drill pilot holes before using screws. Do not hammer nails, since you do not want to cause any unnecessary vi-

brations at this point. If you must nail, also drill fine pilot holes and gently tap in brads, pins or finishing nails as required. If the case inserts are not too large, they can be fastened in place with double-sided foam tape; press the thin panels in place firmly. Next, place case pedestals, attach cradles or mounts on which objects are to be placed and install all remaining labels, following the drawings of the case mock-ups. Hang paintings or framed objects on the large display panels, again taking care not to jostle the large panel.

Before installing the objects you may need to clean them. Check the lenders instructions on what you can and cannot do. To give greater stability to vases and other fragile containers place a cloth bag filled with sand inside.

After the objects and case interiors have been cleaned, the case is ready to be closed. However, before installing the glass, some institutions go through the ritual of photographing the case and its contents for record keeping and public relations purposes. It is much easier to photograph the case and its contents without glass. We mention this for whatever it is worth.

Clean both sides of the glass with ammonia and water. This is the cheapest and best cleaning solution. Prepared window cleaners sometimes leave the glass with a fine greasy film on which dust has a tendency to settle. If you use a plastic sheet, such as Plexiglas or perspex, use a cleaner and anti-static recommended by the manufacturer. Install the glass, wearing white cotton gloves.

■ Freestanding Exhibitions

If you are installing a large exhibition, you will probably have both wall-hung and freestanding elements. We are recommending certain procedures to simplify the process and eliminate some of the chaos generally associated with such an installation. Make sure you have enough help and that every person is assigned specific tasks.

After all the wall-hung panels and cases have been installed, clear the center of the exhibit area of work tables, tools, supplies and refuse.

Depending upon the kind of structural system you plan to use, some elements or parts of your exhibit system can be preassembled prior to moving them into the area. When the gallery is

Figure 99 Placing the Units

Using the scale floor plan, a steel tape measure and a roll of masking tape, plot and locate the freestanding units in the gallery by placing small pieces of masking tape on the floor for each. Double check the measurements since it is easier to change a few pieces of tape than it is to move a large, assembled structure. Have on hand the tools, tool cart and at least one ladder.

prepared, move in the structural elements, partially assembled or disassembled, whichever way is easier and more convenient. Do not forget to bring in the connecting devices. If possible, erect first the structures farthest from the entrance so you do not block the gallery when moving in the balance of the structural system.

☐ *Attaching Panels and Cases*
After the complete structural system is erected in the exhibit area and all components fastened together so there is no danger of collapse, the panels and cases can be moved into place. Following their code numbers, place them in the proper location, then fasten them to the structure.

In some instances, a panel and a case can be fastened by the same connector, so make sure you have enough hands to assist with this task.

Take care that each panel and case is installed with a minimum of unnecessary movement so as not to cause damage or move the structure out of alignment. Make sure that the hands of all work crew members are clean during this process, and inspect panels and cases for fingerprints and smudges.

Small mirrors, cut to the exact size, can also be installed if the rear, side or bottom of an object has design features that cannot normally be seen when given a standard mount.

Figure 100   Turntables

Another way in which all sides of an object can be displayed is to insert a small turntable inside a pedestal by cutting a hole in its top. Variable-speed turntables are available at an electric supply house. Make sure that the speed of rotation is not too fast; 20 to 30 seconds for one rotation is enough. Test this first before it is installed.

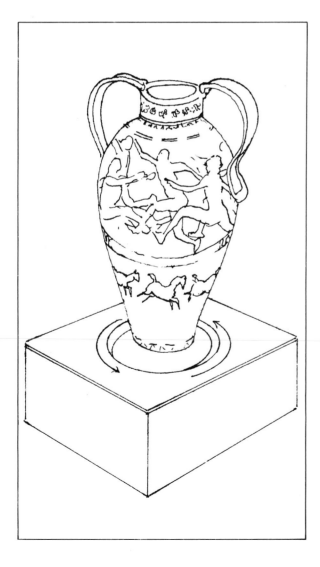

□ *Mounting Labels*

When all cases and panels are in place, you are ready to mount the headings and label copy. Follow directions for painting and installing three-dimensional letters described earlier on page 94. Some minor adjustments may be needed in order to accommodate object replacements. Or you might change your mind when the objects are seen together. If time permits, you can even rearrange case interiors and mount labels in the workroom before bringing the case into the gallery. However, objects should be removed from the cases when you move them to the gallery. *Never move a case with loose objects in it*. Non-breakable objects can be wired to panels and case backs in your workroom and then moved to the gallery.

   Some labels and most objects will have to be installed after the panels and cases are attached to the structural system in the exhibit area. You will have to judge what is feasible to do in advance, and where; however, the care and protection of valuables should always be foremost in mind. The less they are handled, the less chance there is of something being broken or damaged unintentionally. If your help is non-professional, such as volunteers or students, even more care must be taken. One professional staff member should be responsible for all objects and only that person be allowed to handle them.

□ *Adding the Objects*

After all panels, cases and furniture have been installed and the area has been cleaned again, it is time to bring the objects into the gallery. Retain the padded work table but remove anything that might get in the way. Exclude visitors from the gallery when you handle the objects; this is a precaution that should be strictly enforced because it is human nature to want to touch a valuable object. If unauthorized persons are kept out, the chances of an accident or theft are minimized.

   Always install large objects, and those located at the rear of a case, first. Then add medium-sized ones and, finally, the very small. If textiles are contained in a case, these should be put in first, and secured. If items like glass, silver or porcelain are smudged, ask the lenders what is recommended for cleaning. Also, if drilling is to be done or brads to be hammered, do it in an empty case.

It may be necessary, as mentioned earlier, to install labels after some objects have already been inserted. If so, position the labels with masking tape or mark the location in pencil at one of the corners. Then remove the objects and place them on the work table. Glue, nail or foam-tape the label in place. Clean the case again and return the objects.

Some large, unbalanced objects for display on a pedestal must be firmly secured to prevent them from tipping (Figure 101). For support, use an object-mount cradle or armature at the back or side, bolted or screwed to the pedestal. Most objects that need this come equipped with the device. It is only necessary to fasten it to a pedestal.

If the object is openly displayed, erect a barrier to prevent visitors from touching it. This could be a rope, a wooden rail or large sheets of glass or plastic clamped together. If the pedestal is free-standing, secure it to the floor with double-face foam tape.

After all objects and labels are in place, the case interior should be brushed again (by the professional installer, not cleaning staff) to remove bits of lint or sawdust.

Figure 101   Pedestal Supports

A metal cradle or an armature is attached to the pedestal (a). Drill small holes in the top of the pedestal on which to rest the cradle. For the armature, drill holes and insert interior fastening.

Some exposed objects with a base or lip require a number of "Z" fastening plates padded with felt and screwed to the top of the pedestal. The "Z" plates can be cut out of strap iron or sheet brass with a hacksaw, with a hole drilled, then bent to shape in a vise. Paint them the same color as the pedestal, then glue felt to the part that touches the object. The fit should be firm but not too tight (b).

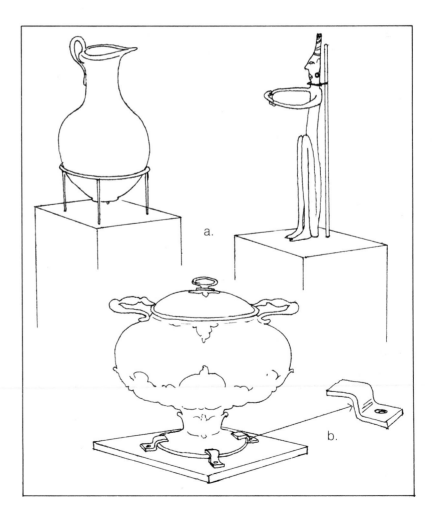

■ Handling the Objects[*]

□ *Paintings*

1. Do not move or carry more than one painting at a time, regardless of size. Always carry a painting with one hand underneath and the other at the side, both at points where the frame is solid. Never carry a painting by the top or by the stretcher.

2. Large (i.e., large enough to be awkward for one person) paintings should always be carried by two persons.

3. Try not to stack paintings one on top of the other.

4. Separate paintings with a composition sheet (foamcore, cardboard or a compboard, etc.) if stacking is absolutely unavoidable. Stack the largest painting first, followed by smaller ones in descending order, with no more than five paintings in any one stack. Each composition sheet must cover completely the larger of the two paintings it separates.

5. Paintings standing on the floor must rest on pads or padded wooden strips.

6. If paintings are moved on a side truck, glass truck or dolly, separate the paintings as above and rest them on a pad. Paintings should not extend beyond the edge of the truck or dolly.

7. Do not move large, heavy paintings on a side truck unless the truck's supporting framework is high enough; that is, at least two-thirds of the height of the painting. The weight of the painting must be borne by the frame resting against the truck support; it should never be borne by the stretcher alone.

8. Before the truck is moved, lash the painting in place using pads at the points where the rope touches the frame. Two persons must accompany each loaded moving hand truck. One person must be experienced in the handling of art objects.

*Prime source: *The Care and Handling of Art Objects* by Robert P. Sugden, Metropolitan Museum of Art, New York, 1946.

9. When dismantling an exhibition, do not remove hanging devices—wires, hooks, etc., from the frames or panels unless otherwise instructed by the organizer.

10. Avoid direct contact with painted surfaces at all times. Do not attempt to remove slight scratches, rubbed spots or dirt marks with your hand, a cloth, or by any other means. Where varnish on a painting is in poor condition, even gentle pressure will leave a mark that may call for treatment of the entire surface.

11. Wear white cotton gloves to avoid damaging finger marks when working with light-colored, matte-finish or gilded frames. Clean hands are not enough in this case as perspiration spots so easily spoil a frame's appearance.

12. Report any damage that appears to be of recent origin, no matter how slight it seems to be. Get in the habit of examining every painting to determine condition.

13. If paint flakes or frame parts become detached, save all the pieces. Repairs are much easier if all parts are available.

□ *Small Objects* (*ceramics, glass, enamels, etc.*)

1. Never handle any object unnecessarily. Always work with proper supervision.

2. Move only one object at a time and carry it with one hand underneath. Unpack over a padded table so that detached parts will not be lost or damaged.

3. Never lift small, fragile objects by handles, rims or other projections for these parts may have been broken before and repaired. Hold the body of the piece gently but firmly. Check each object in and out of the padded tray in your gallery cart when it consists of more than one part.

4. Always use padded trays for moving small objects. Do not move them by hand except for placement in trays. Use sufficient cotton or padding within the tray to prevent contact of one object with other objects. Whenever possible,

place objects so that they do not project above the top of the tray.

5. Make sure that hands are clean. Use gloves or tissue when handling objects with glazed, polished metal, or other highly finished surfaces since such materials show finger marks, which are difficult to remove. Apply this rule to matte finishes and painted decorations as well. Smooth-surfaced objects are hard to handle with gloves or tissue; therefore, extra care is necessary.

6. Do not move trays by hand from one part of the building to another. Use a gallery cart. Speed and jarring motion should be strictly avoided. Take time to do the job properly.

7. When moving small sculptures, always place them on pads and make sure they are carefully supported so their weight is evenly distributed. Leave space between objects to avoid chipping and scratching.

8. Ivories and small wood carvings are affected by sudden changes of atmosphere; therefore, do not work with such pieces near open windows or doors, particularly during winter months or wet weather.

9. Arms, armor and most metal objects are subject to damage in many ways. Such objects should not be handled by inexperienced persons. Always handle with gloves as finger marks cause rust. Also, avoid exposure to dampness or high humidity.

10. Jewelry is usually very fragile; therefore, never place cotton in direct contact with it. Cotton can catch on delicate parts and may loosen settings, causing loss of stones. Wrap jewelry first in tissue and then in cotton, if added protection is needed. Ivories, enamels and old glass should be treated in the same way, wrapped first in tissue, and then in cotton. There must be strict supervision when working with jeweled objects.

□ *Large Sculpture*

1. The movement of large sculpture is a technical problem. Do not attempt it with too little help or without competent direction. Haste in handling may result in injury to the handlers or damage to the object.

2. Do not carry heavy sculpture by hand, even if you are able to lift it. Sculpture should always be moved on padded trucks, supported and, if necessary, tied to prevent harmful movement while the truck or dolly is in motion.

3. Sculpture should always be examined before handling. Knowing the points of weakness in advance is important to the safe movement of the object. If there are any doubts about how an object is to be moved or handled, call the lender or the organizer for advice.

□ *Woodwork and Furniture*

1. Always move woodwork or furniture on trucks or dollies. Never slide or push such objects along the floor as legs or bases can be easily broken.

2. Always lift chairs under the seat rail, never by the backs or arms. Carry tables and other furniture by the solid parts of their framework, not the ornamentation.

3. Cover upholstered furniture in transit, as delicate fabrics are difficult to clean. Do not touch the upholstery on the arms, seats or backs of chairs or sofas. Cover upholstery with clean sheets until the exhibit is ready to open.

4. Never stack furniture when moving it.

5. Unlocked drawers, cabinet doors, folding table tops and all other movable parts must be held in place to prevent damage in transit. Tie these parts to the main part of the furniture, using pads where the rope touches the wood.

6. Remove marble tops for transit and transport them in a vertical position on a side truck. Do not carry marble horizontally since it may break of its own weight.

7. Wood paneling is seldom as strong as it looks. Sufficient help and proper supervision are needed in carrying it.

As with all objects being unpacked and moved to your exhibit area, save all parts which may have become broken or detached. Also, avoid haste in handling objects and avoid speed with hand trucks loaded with objects. Report every bit of damage that appears to be new.

□ *Tapestries, Rugs and Large Textiles*

1. Never lift mounted textiles so that all of the weight is borne by the fabric alone. Use the supporting bar, roller or stretcher for lifting and handling.

2. Cover and protect textiles until they are ready to be installed. Retain and mark the cover so the same one can be used when repacking or storing.

3. Avoid stretching, tugging and pulling. Textiles that seem to be sturdy are frequently old, worn or repaired and they can tear easily. Use the same care in handling contemporary textiles that you use with older ones.

4. Remove screw eyes, wires and other projections (unless told otherwise by the lender) before rolling textiles on supporting bars. Roll tapestries, large textiles and rugs evenly, avoiding wrinkling and creasing. If the textile has a lining, roll the lined material face out.

5. Rugs, tapestries and large textiles on wrapped rollers should not be picked up by one person or grasped at the middle of the bar. Use two persons, one supporting each end, for greater protection while moving a roll of textile.

6. Do not pile rolled or folded textiles one on top of another unless it is absolutely necessary. This practice results in broken threads which are virtually impossible to repair.

7. Observe strict safety rules when installing and removing large textiles from exhibitions. There should always be another person at the foot of each ladder to steady it.

□ *Costumes and Small Textiles*

1. Handle mounted textiles by the stretcher or frame. Slight pressure on the fabric can cause serious damage.

2. Do not fold textiles, laces, costumes, etc., unless given permission to do so. If it is necessary to fold them, place tissue paper in the folds to prevent creasing.

3. Clean hands are essential in working with textiles. Many fabrics are so fragile that cleaning is virtually impossible.

4. Cover costumed mannequins until the exhibit is ready to open. Also leave covers on when the mannequins are moved. Always lift the mannequin by its framework when moving it in order to avoid soiling or tearing the costume.

5. After removing textiles and costumes from exhibitions, be sure that all pins are removed to prevent possible rust stains as well as blood stains from scratched fingers. This procedure should be followed also for contemporary textiles and costumes.

□ *Drawings, Watercolors, Prints, Miniatures and Rare Books*

Works in this group are among the most fragile and easily damaged in the museum. Treat these objects with care and consideration. Do not handle them unless it is your job to do so, and then only if you are experienced.

1. Handle as little as possible and only with clean hands. Never touch material of this kind with wet, sticky or dirty fingers. If your hands perspire, wear white cotton gloves.

2. When moving unmounted material, lift each sheet by the upper corners so it hangs free without buckling. Use great care to avoid bending, cracking and tearing. Support such works on clean cardboard when carrying them by hand, or carry them in glassine envelopes.

3. Never stack prints or drawings one on top of another unless they are matted or are separated

by cellophane, glassine or tissue paper. Do not allow newsprint, printed matter, sized papers, or other paper of poor quality to come into direct contact with the objects. Always cover works awaiting installation, framing or transportation with acid-free tissue paper to exclude dust and dirt.

4. Do not permit works on paper to be shuffled or rubbed against each other. It is extremely difficult to repair damage done in this manner.

5. Do not expose prints, drawings, watercolors and illuminated manuscripts to direct or indirect sunlight or to fluorescent lamps (unless they have been fitted with a UV filter), whether on exhibition, awaiting installation or in storage.

6. Many book and manuscript bindings that may appear to be in good condition are actually fragile. Never take a chance. Always handle these objects with extreme care. Leather bindings and old leather objects are easily stained. Do not handle these objects unless it is necessary.

7. Turn the pages on old books from the upper, outer corners, if and when it is necessary to open the book and turn the pages. Moistened fingers are extremely harmful to paper.

8. Open books gently so as not to crack the spine of the bindings. And never try to make an open book lie flat. If on display a book should be placed on a cradle to protect the binding. Never stack open books one on top of another and never place open books face down. Do not stand books on their front edges, whether on tables, padded trucks or shelves. Old books should always lie flat.

Always seek professsional advice from the lender on how to display old books and manuscripts. If the books are from your own collection, consult a librarian.

The same care indicated for art objects should apply to historic objects, ethnographic and archaeological objects, and to delicate natural history specimens such as insects, eggs, bird and mammal mounts, shells, botanical models and fragile geological specimens.

■ Temperature, Humidity and Light

With few exceptions, most museums and galleries in this country are subjected to seasonal changes in temperature and humidity. This, coupled with the continuing world energy shortage, poses a major cause of concern for our collective cultural properties. To this we can also add the chemical pollutants in our air. All of this combined can lead to immediate damage and long-term destruction of our collections.

Although museums and other cultural institutions are exempt from federal guidelines governing heating and cooling restrictions, there is still cause for concern because of a possible energy shortage. Most major museums and organizers will not lend entire exhibitions or even objects unless they are assured that specific environmental standards will be adhered to. The National Conservation Advisory Council endorses the following guidelines:*

1. Institutions responsible for the preservation of cultural patrimony must be given special consideration when energy priorities are established.

2. The primary need is to maintain humidity and temperature as steady as possible. When major changes in temperature and humidity unavoidably occur, special efforts must be made to control the rate of change so it will only take place gradually over a period of at least one week.

3. Should it become absolutely impossible to maintain accepted environmental standards (50 percent relative humidity, ± 5 percent, and 65 degrees F, ± 5 degrees), every effort must be made to maintain relative humidity within a range of not less than 40 percent (winter) or more than 60 percent (summer). Temperatures should be kept with a range of not less than 55 degrees (winter) or more than 80 degrees F (summer).

*National Conservation Advisory Council, ''Statement on the Control of Environmental Conditions for Preservation of Cultural Property in Situations of Energy Shortage,'' December, 1977.

4.   Certain classes of materials, such as microfilm, motion-picture film, and other photographic negative materials require special levels of temperature and humidity other than those described above.

Any institution contemplating a program of traveling exhibitions or loan objects must have some system of control of environment and air. While some shows might have different optimal environmental constraints (for instance, Japanese lacquer requires a higher humidity), most containing museum-quality objects will require a relative humidity of 50 percent ± 5 percent and a temperature of 65 degrees F ± 5 degrees, as mentioned earlier.

If you intend to upgrade or install a new air-handling system, provide also for an air-filtering system to filter out solid particles and chemical pollutants. This is especially critical for institutions in urban areas.

With lenders of valuable objects becoming more and more conservation-minded, it is essential that you do, too.

A number of free publications dealing with conservation, the protection of collections and energy issues can be obtained from the Energy Information Clearing House, Box 241, New York, New York 10024 or from the American Association of Museums, 1055 Thomas Jefferson Street, N.W., Washington, DC 20007.

When considering lighting, remember that all light sources produce ultraviolet radiation in varying amounts, which can cause photochemical damage to an object. The most damaging is sunlight, less damaging is fluorescent light, with the least harmful being incandescent light. It is important to note that any light, whether strong or weak, will produce some damage; how much, is a matter of degree. An object can be damaged from a weak light if it is exposed to that light source for a long time; likewise, an object can be damaged from a strong light source if exposed for a short duration. Damage caused by light cannot be reversed. Faded colors and brittle materials cannot be restored to their original condition. Therefore,

the potentially damaging effects of light, ultraviolet radiation as well as heat, must be removed. For elimination of ultraviolet, filters should be used for all fluorescent lamps. A UF-1 Rohm & Haas filter, in the form of a flexible transparent plastic tube to slip over a fluorescent tube or in rigid sheet form (which can be cut to any size) is strongly recommended.

Daylight should be totally eliminated or strongly filtered for all but certain exhibits where reflected or direct sunlight will not harm the objects (stone sculptures, machinery, and metal objects).

Ultraviolet radiation is far more hazardous than visible light. If, however, footcandle levels are sufficiently high, such shorter wavelength visible radiation may also become significantly hazardous, even if all untraviolet radiation is filtered out. See page 00 for recommended footcandle or lux values of illumination.

■ Cleaning

During the installation planning and design and fabrication phases, always keep in mind the problem of exhibition maintenance. Any public area, and your exhibit installation is no exception, will receive continued punishment—airborne dust and dirt everywhere, wet and muddy feet on the floor, greasy finger and nose prints on the glass or plastic case fronts, graffiti on walls, panels and cases, dropped paper and much more. Therefore, your installation should be designed so that general cleaning and maintenance can be undertaken with a minimum of effort. Avoid fussy detailing in your panels and case design; try not to create culs-de-sac in your exhibit layout where dirt and dust can easily gather. Design your cases and panels and their layout so that maintenance people can clean around the cases easily without bumping or jarring them. Also, it is advisable to save at least a pint of each paint color used in the exhibit for retouching, should the need arise.

Schedule cleaning of your exhibit every day before the area is open to the public. First, clean walls of hand marks and graffiti, then dust ledges and flat areas. Next, clean floors with either a sweeping compound (to eliminate dust) mop or vacuum, depending upon the finish. Finally, clean glass and plastic. Make periodic inspections of the gallery during the day to catch dirty glass and graffiti, especially if the exhibition is popular. Dirt or graffiti appearing on walls, panels or cases, should be cleaned immediately as dirt and disorder invite more of the same.

Since public areas take a good deal of public abuse, they must be cleaned regularly. It is important to use materials that will wear well, so your exhibit does not look two years old after only two weeks.

A neat, clean environment instills respect. If you create a feeling of quality through craftsmanship, even in the simplest panel construction, application of paint on walls and pedestals, neatness in installing cutout letters and labels, and thoughtfulness in installing three-dimensional objects, the overall effect will evoke positive reactions from visitors. □

Chapter 7

Security

7

Security

■ Security

Over the past decade, there has been an increase in the loss and deterioration of the world's art and cultural legacy through theft, fire, vandalism and negligence. Because of this unfortunate reality, it is the duty of everyone who mounts an exhibition containing valuable objects to familiarize himself with museum security and to provide a safe environment for those objects. See page 167 for a bibliography on the subject with special reference to Robert Tillotson's book, *Museum Security.*

Some organizers, very much aware of the problem of security, have classified each of their traveling exhibitions into one of three types of security requirements to which an exhibition lessee must adhere. They are 1) high security, 2) moderate security, and 3) limited security. If you book a traveling exhibition and the organizer has not spelled out the security requirements in sufficient detail, you have the responsibility to find out what kind of security you must provide.

Using the Smithsonian Institution Traveling Exhibition Service's security classifications as a guideline for other traveling exhibitions or for exhibitions you might organize yourself, they are:

1.   A High Security Exhibition
These contain objects extremely valuable or sensitive to light, humidity and temperature. This includes original art and antiques such as paintings, sculpture, rare prints, drawings and manuscripts; certain objects made of wood; porcelain; certain textiles; objects of gold, silver and objects containing precious metals and jewels; most archaeological treasures and other highly valuable items.

The Lessee: A qualified institution, i.e., a museum or a well-established gallery.

Space: A gallery with limited access, preferably a room with one entrance also used as an exit. An open mall, hallway or lounge area is not acceptable.

Protection:
a)   Trained professional security personnel in sufficient number and in shifts to adequately protect the exhibition's contents.
b)   Night guards and/or an electronic security system
c)   Provisions to prevent the public from touching wall-hung objects through an appropriate hanging system, the use of barriers, platforms and/or guard supervision.
d)   Locked glass cases for small objects. In some instances laminated safety glass. Plastic or Plexiglas cases are not acceptable for high security exhibitions.
e)   The handling of objects only by a trained professional, i.e., a curator or a museum registrar or conservator.

Environmental Controls:
a)   Temperature and light control are required for all exhibits in this category. Humidity control is required for some and desired for all others.
b)   Fire system and other protection devices ac-

cording to local ordinances.

Other Considerations:
a)   Informing local law enforcement agency of the arrival of the exhibition and the length of its stay.
b)   Periodic visits to the gallery by local police.
c)   Safe area where the contents can be unpacked and temporary secure area where they can be stored before installation.
d)   Limited access by authorized personnel only to storage area and exhibit gallery while objects are being installed.

2.   A Moderate Security Exhibition
Various exhibitions that contain original art works, prints and graphics, original specimens, artifacts, or original photographs are classified as moderate security exhibitions.

The Lessee: All qualified galleries.

Space: Limited access, a gallery-type area. An open mall, hallway or lounge area is not acceptable.

Protection:
a)   Professional guards, or other trained persons whose *sole* duty is the supervision of the exhibition.
b)   Locked glass cases or secure plastic or Plexiglas must be screwed to wall or base cabinet, not just resting on top of a unit.
c)   The exhibit area must be locked and secure during closing hours. Alarm and/or guards during night hours are preferred but not required.
d)   Handling of objects must be done by a person trained in the handling of museum objects, e.g., curator, registrar, conservator, preparator or exhibit technician.

Environmental Controls:
a)   Temperature and light control are required. Humidity control is desired.
b)   Fire protection according to local ordinances.

Other Considerations:
a)   Safe area where the exhibition can be unpacked and temporary secure area where objects can be stored before installation.
b)   Limited access by authorized personnel only

to storage area and exhibit gallery while objects are being installed.

3.   A Limited Security Exhibition
These are either panels containing no original materials, or displays of artifacts, photography, or children's art that are considered less of a security risk.

The Lessee: Any qualified organization or gallery.

Space: Exhibits may be shown in a gallery or lounge area, but preferably not in hallways. Exhibits are not to be installed outdoors, in tents or in temporary buildings, unless they are specifically designed for such spaces.

Protection:
a)   Supervision by guard, volunteer, student or receptionist. Someone must watch the exhibition at all times but may be performing other duties as well. No exhibit is to be left unattended at any time while open to the public. Even panel and photo exhibits are sometimes the object of theft or vandalism.
b)   The exhibit area must be locked and secure during closing hours.

Environmental Controls:
a)   Direct sunlight should be diffused or eliminated to prevent fading of panels and photographs.
b)   Fire protection according to local ordinances is required.

■ Guards

Guards and attendants can be strategically stationed not only to protect the exhibition's contents, but also to answer questions and give information about the related activities. In a sense, they take the part of the hosts and can perform a valuable public-relations function but only to the degree that this does not interfere with their primary job, namely guarding the exhibition. Regardless of whether you hire outside security professionals or use your own in-house personnel, guards should be trained in the special problems faced by museums and galleries. Of prime concern are:

1. Strategy for protecting the most valuable objects.
2. Attitude toward the public.
3. Fire and panic control.
4. Knowledge of first aid.
5. Familiarity with the layout of the gallery and/or building.
6. Understanding what is and what is not permissible within the law.
7. Special indoctrination by your local police and fire departments.
8. Ability to answer questions concerning related programs, such as films, lectures and general education. Each guard should be given a calendar of events.

When hiring, use an employment application form specifically for museum guards and explore in an interview the prospect's attitudes toward people and museums. Look for evidence of antisocial behavior. Temperament, too, is important. Guards should be able to act calmly and authoritatively in emergencies; they should be able to sustain their powers of observation through long hours of duty; they should be able to deal with children and unruly teenagers firmly and with understanding; and they should not get impatient with endless questions. Past experience in a related job is often evidence of a temperamental affinity for the type of work required.

■ Mechanical and Electronic Devices

If an institution is committed to an annual program of six to eight changing exhibitions, many of them high security, it should seriously consider installing a security system for the gallery. There is a multitude of mechanical and electronic systems from which to choose. These include smoke and heat detectors, vibration detectors, photoelectric eyes, door and window alarms, closed-circuit television, glass-breaking sensors, contact mats, microwave motion detectors, ultrasonic motion detectors, passive infrared devices, weight sensors, vibration switches, and many, many others.

This is a complex subject. We can only make you aware that these systems are desirable and that professional assistance should be relied upon. With the help of a security specialist, your exhibition and storage requirements can be secured according to your specifications. Compare systems and devices proposed by the consultant and talk with users to see if they function as they should. The final selection may consist of a combination of devices from different manufacturers. Selection criteria to remember are:

1. The system should be tested after it is installed. A guarantee with periodic testing should be included in a contract with the supplier/installer.
2. The system should be installed with precision and neatness.
3. The system should operate simply and not require a degree in electronics to be understood.
4. It should require a minimum of maintenance.
5. The equipment should be guaranteed.
6. The false-alarm rate should be low or non-existent.
7. The system and its circuits should be tamper-proof. Keep a circuit diagram in a safe place.
8. Continuous current should be provided for the security system. In case of a power failure, have a reserve emergency power available for at least 48 hours.*

We recommend that, before talking with a security consultant, you draft an outline of the kinds of protection you need based upon the kinds of exhibits you regularly schedule. If you use a variety from wall-hung paintings to freestanding cases of decorative arts and jewelry, note this information. Also, prepare a breakdown of attendance figures, indicating peak and low attendance by day, week and month. Include a description of the audience. The security consultant will want to know everything there is to know about your op-

* Prime source: Tillotson, Robert G. *Museum Security*, International Council of Museums, Paris, 1977

eration so he can provide the best possible system.

■ Protective Barriers

One can go only so far in protecting objects without making the exhibition area look like an armed camp. Small items of value, of course, must be placed in locked glass cases; large valuables can be protected by alarms and sheets of glass or plastic. But there are many large objects that need only to be protected by a physical or psychological distance. Period furniture, costumes, farm equipment, large ethnographic objects, historic technological objects and others can be separated from visitors by velvet ropes, railings, plants or raised platforms. These psychological barriers are not foolproof, they are only a deterrent. Anyone determined to touch or vandalize an object will have to scale the barrier and with some effort reach his target. It is therefore up to your guard force to anticipate a visitor with that irresistible urge. It is essential that your guard force be trained as careful observers and be able to recognize certain peculiar mannerisms and characteristics of a potential wrongdoer. Security experts agree that alert guards are very effective in preventing theft or damage.

■ Safety

Every public space, whether it is a large museum or a small gallery, should have a written policy covering accident prevention. However, a written accident prevention policy is useless unless it is practiced and enforced. Periodic surveys of the building and grounds should be made and all hazardous conditions remedied or clearly posted. You and your staff should also arrange regular safety meetings.

The following is a list to consider:

1.   Fire alarms should be clearly marked.

2.   Fire extinguishers should be readily accessible in public as well as in non-public areas. Your staff should know where they are and how to use them.

3.   Do not let a gallery become overcrowded. Since it is a public space you should know the maximum density.

4.   Repair loose carpeting so people will not trip and fall. Anti-skid mats should be used on wet days for slippery floors.

5.   Look out for physical hazards such as trailing cords or sharp angles.

6.   Entrance and stairways should be marked and well illuminated.

7.   Exits and emergency doors should be well marked.

8.   Electric tools should contain safety devices.

9.   Follow workshop safety precautions when using tools. No one should use shop tools unless he or she is proficient.

10.   Always keep the workshop clean.

11.   Store inflammable materials, especially paints and thinners, in explosion-proof lockers.

12.   Throw dirty rags in special covered waste containers.

13.   Use yellow extension cords in a workshop and gallery so they can be seen.

14.   Always have two persons use a ladder; one to climb and one to hold and steady it.

15.   Establish a first-aid routine and always have a first-aid kit handy during fabrication and installation periods. A first-aid kit should also be available for gallery personnel when the exhibit is open. You, your staff and volunteers should be schooled in first aid.

16.   Post emergency telephone numbers next to telephones.

17.   Smoking should be limited to specific areas only.

18.   Check your exhibit daily to make sure that everything is in working order. If not, make repairs immediately. □

Chapter 8

Evaluation

8

Evaluation

■ Evaluation

There seems to be general agreement among most museum professionals that exhibitions, including traveling ones, should be evaluated for their effectiveness. A few institutions are somewhat reticent because the results could be "ego damaging." We believe that the evaluation process is not a form of punishment but a constructive process whereby we can learn from our mistakes as well as successes. It makes sense to say that the

purpose of an exhibition is to provide pleasure, educate and enlighten visitors by conveying information, increase interest in a particular subject, and reinforce certain beliefs and attitudes. Therefore, if we want to achieve these goals, evaluation can be a valuable tool in showing us how we may improve our performance.

Evaluation can start in the early design phase and continue after the exhibit and related programs are under way. Certain design solutions can be tested in the scale-model stage and then easily changed. If you apply for grant funds for its development and execution, special monies should be designated for evaluation as well as for use in correcting ineffective areas, once testing shows a weakness or lack of communication.

Important questions to answer for putting on more effective exhibits are:*

1. Who makes up the audience? What are they interested in? What are their objectives?

2. What are your objectives? Do you have information to convey, attitudes to change, or both? Has anyone tried to specify them?

3. How best can you reach your own goals and objectives and those of your audience? What content and what media are most appropriate? How much time, money, talent, do you have to work with?

4. Once you decide to put an exhibit together, does it really work? If it doesn't, where is the problem and how can it be fixed? Can you pretest an idea before putting a lot of money into it?

5. What have you learned from your experience that would help yourself and others to do even better the next time? Did you document and share your findings?

Harris Shettel, a leader in testing the effectiveness of exhibits, offers six recommendations that he feels need to be implemented in order to upgrade educational exhibits. They are:

1. Teaching exhibits must have explicitly stated objectives.

2. When you know what you are trying to achieve with a target audience or audiences, you are ready to consider the appropriate content through which to reach your objectives.

* Primary source for discussion on evaluation is Shettel, H.H., "Exhibits: Art Form or Educational Medium?" *Museum News*, Vol. 52, No. 1, 1973.

3. It is essential that careful thought be given to the order in which information is to be learned and to ensure through the exhibit design that this order is followed.

4. One of the most powerful principles to emerge from the general field of behavioral psychology and its application to instruction has been the idea that active participation heightens the acquisition and retention of information.

5. Closely related to participation is reinforcement.

Shettel's recommendations in their combined form can be seen as a means of controlling viewer behavior; that is he suggests that the exhibit be designed so the content is controlled, the sequence is controlled, and an incentive to continue responding to the learning from the exhibit is the end result.

His final recommendation, as a #6, involves "a process that has become an integral part of most programmed instructional materials and other so-called innovative approaches to education: the need to test and revise materials before they are considered ready for public consumption."

All of this testing and analyzing would seem to indicate the need for a considerable amount of time, especially when planning, design and execution time is limited. However, as mentioned earlier, one can test during the early design stage by using exhibit models, photographs of the objects for display and early drafts of label copy. A simple graphics, drawing or painting exhibition can be improved by making sure that label copy identifying the objects as well as describing the cultural context in which they were created is clear, concise and informative. For more didactic (story-telling) exhibitions, the need for testing is even greater.

Since evaluation requires a knowledge of education and psychology, it is a good idea to contact a specialist or a college educational psychologist. He or she may be willing to take on your evaluation as a class project—a "living laboratory" for the students. □

Chapter 9

The Handicapped

9

The Handicapped

■ The Handicapped

Recent federal laws* and other federal regulations now being written provide civil rights for all handicapped citizens, specifically for accessibility to public buildings and for accessibility to cultural programs. These laws require that public schools and cultural institutions receiving federal financial assistance, directly or indirectly, through any federally-funded programs or exhibits (*in toto* or in part), must comply with the legislation. This means that if you have an exhibit that is totally or partially supported with federal monies, it must be accessible to the handicapped through provision of barrier-free architecture (such as ramps or elevators) by which the handicapped can reach the exhibit; and the exhibitor must provide them equal opportunity to the exhibit and its related programs. It also means that if you have lectures, art education programs, studios, displays, performances that are open to the public, these programs and facilities must also be made accessible to the blind, the deaf, persons in wheelchairs and other physically handicapped persons. In other words, the legislation aims to provide accessibility to all cultural programs for the nation's handicapped, roughly 50 million persons.

What you can do to accommodate the handicapped:

1.   Familiarize yourself with the literature available.

2.   Consult with city, county and state agencies concerned with the handicapped.

3.   Consult with educators dedicated to teaching the handicapped.

4.   Form a volunteer group for your institution that would devote itself to organizing and operating programs for the handicapped.

5.   Raise funds to make your building and gallery barrier-free.

6.   Offer workshop programs related to special exhibitions for:

    a.   children with learning disabilities;
    b.   the blind and visually impaired;
    c.   the deaf and hearing impaired.

7.   Rehabilitate your restrooms to accommodate wheelchair users.

8.   Install braille indications in your elevator(s).

9.   Lower some telephones and some drinking fountains.

10.   Make sure that there are curb cuts for wheelchairs on the streets near your facility.

11.   For the deaf, provide scripts or abstracts of audio-visual presentations; provide a volunteer interpreter for films and lectures.

12.   For the blind, provide a cassette tour of the exhibit or braille description. Install special "hands-on" objects for the blind to feel.

13.   Make aisles wide enough to accommodate wheelchairs.

14.   Coat ramps with non-slip surfaces.

15.   Install a rotating collection of touchable museum objects in a permanent gallery, manned by trained volunteers for the blind as well as sighted visitors.

*P.L. 94-142 and P.L. 93-112, section 504

Chapter 10

The Toolbox

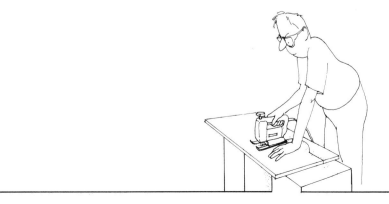

10

The Toolbox

■ The Toolbox

All museums and galleries own hand tools and at least a few power tools. The larger the institution the more extensive the tool collection; many contain a workshop, maintenance shop or exhibition preparation room.

All installation work involves the use of hand tools at some point—to dismantle the show and to close the shipping crates, to mention only a few. In complex displays, or when adding pieces of your own, you may fabricate panels and cases using simple power tools. It is important to select the right ones and handle them correctly.

Tools are a long-term investment. When buying, always buy the best. Store them in a toolbox

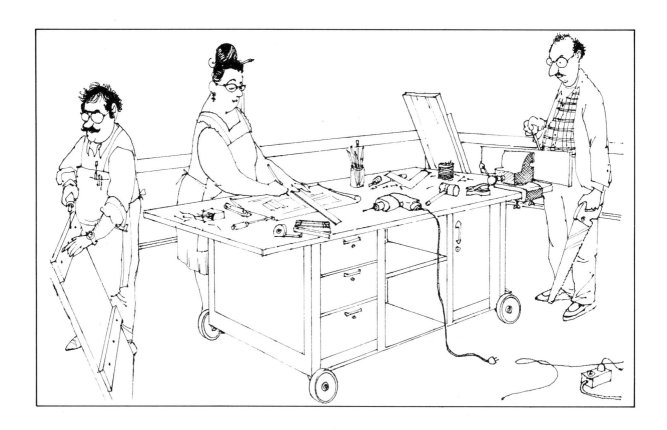

Figure 103   Workbench on Wheels

For an institution with many exhibition needs, a good investment is a wheeled workbench that can be moved into the gallery. It should contain locks on the drawers and doors.

locked in a secure place. When maintained and used with care, they should last more than one lifetime.

When it comes to tools and equipment there are those who thrive on the mere possession of hardware with "Midas-like" obsession; we do not belong to this group. The list of basic tools may seem extensive, but we have included only those that will assist you in achieving a more professional product. Before setting to work, it is always wise to go through your equipment to make sure that nails, screws, pins, sandpaper, glue, etc., are plentiful.

Listed below is a basic tool kit that every gallery or small museum should possess. Pictured on the next pages are the range of tools used in the preparation of an exhibition.

Basic Hand Tools and Equipment

Safety goggles
Metal rule (24-inch)
Steel measuring tape (12-foot)
Steel measuring tape (50-foot)
Crosscut saw
Hacksaw (with extra blades)
Backsaw and miter box
Keyhole saw
Hammer (claw)
Nail set
Nail punch
Assorted screws (metal and wood)
Assorted bolts and nuts
Assorted nails
Assorted screw eyes
Assorted washers
Hand drill and bits
Brace and bits
Awl
Three regular screwdrivers (three sizes)
One Phillips screwdriver
Adjustable wrench
Mat knife (with extra blades)
X-Acto knife (with extra blades)
Slip joint pliers
Side cutting pliers
Needle nose pliers
Large roll of picture wire (several different weights)
Medium sized roll of fine copper wire
Rafter square
Combination square

Carpenter's level (36 inches long)
Torpedo level
Carpenter's compass/divider
Assorted sandpapers
4-in-hand rasp file
Half round file
Rattail file
Combination plier wrench
Channel-type pliers
Box of dressmaker's pins (with rounded heads)
Crowbar or wrecking bar (two sizes)
3½-inch jaw vise (with aluminum inserts for the jaws)
Collection of C-clamps
Metal snips
Heavy duty stapler with extra staples
Pipe clamps (four) plus sets of two lengths of pipe
Dust pan with hand brush
Three animal hair brushes (1, 2, and 4-inch) for cleaning
Wire stripper
Roll of electrician's tape
1-inch roll of masking tape
1-inch roll of 3M heavy duty double-faced foam tape
Scraper
Soldering gun
Solder
Solder flux
Stiff wire brush

Soft wire brush
Palette knife
Putty knife
Nylon band clamp
6-inch spring clamps (eight)
Set of three wood chisels
Roll of monofilament (clear) fishing line, 20 lb. test
White glue
Tube of Duco cement
Rubber cement
Solvent
Rubber cement pickup
Thumb tacks
Pushpins
Paper clips
Ball of twine
White cotton gloves
Glass cleaner
Plexiglas cleaner
Brass cleaner
Soft cloth rags
Pail
Plastic sponges
Assorted magic markers
Assorted erasers (pink, art gum, kneaded)
Erasing shield
36-inch steel straight-edge
Mat board cutter with extra blades
Cutting board
Needles and spools of various color threads

Power tools (optional)

⅜-inch electric variable

speed reversable drill and set of drill bits*
Three-prong heavy duty extension cord (at least 20 feet long)
Electric saber saw with extra blades
Portable electric power saw
Electric sander

*Some galleries and museums strongly adhere to a battery-powered drill. They recommend a ¼-inch reversible, variable speed battery unit which is cordless and rechargeable. This drill comes with standard drill bits as well as a screwdriver bit.

Miscellaneous Equipment

36-inch roll of brown craft paper and holder
Three-step ladder
6-foot aluminum step ladder
Four saw horses
Two dollies
Two to four work tables (with pads)
Two gallery carts (with pads)
Glass dolly/cart
Flat truck (with pads)

125

Figure 104   Hammers

a. Curved claw hammer—
general carpentry work and nail
removal. (Always place a wood
block under the hammer head to
prevent marring when removing
nails.) b. Ball peen hammer—
metalwork and, particularly,
shaping metal. c. Tack
hammer—tacks fabrics, such as
upholstery or cloth, around a
panel. d. Mallets (wood or
plastic)—drive chisels. e. Mallets
(rubber)—assembling or disas-
sembling many metal structural
systems without marring the finish.

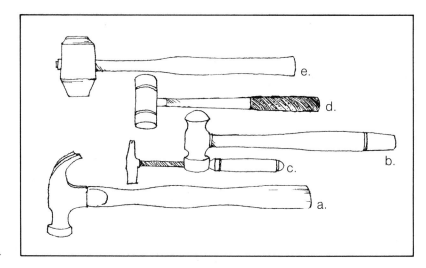

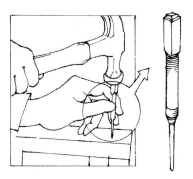

Figure 105   Nail Sets

Nail sets—drive finishing
nailheads below the surface of
the work for concealment.

Figure 106   Saws

a. Crosscut saw—cuts lumber.
(The greater the number of teeth
per inch the smoother the cut.)
b. Backsaw—joint cutting, in association with a miter box.
c. Coping saw—cuts small
diameter curves. d. Compass or
Keyhole saw—cuts curves or
starts from a bored hole.
e. Hacksaw—cuts metal and pipe.

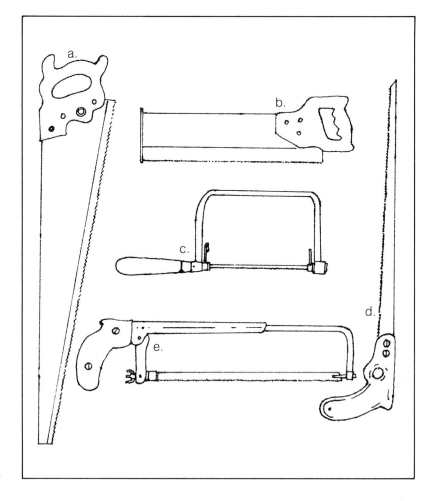

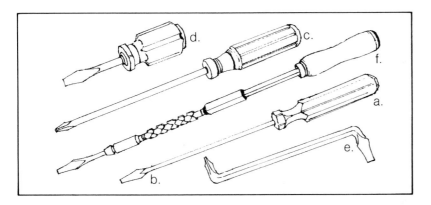

Figure 108 Pliers

Like all specialized tools, pliers come in a variety of shapes and sizes for use in specific tasks. a. Slip-joint pliers—normal and wide-jaw openings. b. Linesman's pliers—heavy duty wire cutting and splicing. c. Long-nose pliers—shaping wire and thin metal; sometimes for cutting. d. Diagonal-cutting pliers—cutting only, they have no gripping jaws. e. End-cutting pliers—cutting wire, nails, brads as well as pulling nails. f. Channel-lock pliers—adjust for large jaw openings and will grip almost any shape with long handle leverage. g. Combination plier-wrench—functions as pliers, wrench or vise. Jaws can be straight for general work or curved for work on round objects like pipe or tubing.

Figure 107 Screwdrivers

These should be matched to screw size and screw type; blades must fit the screw slot. Before starting a screw, pre-drill a hole with drill and drill bit slightly smaller than the screw, or use an awl or a gimlet to punch a hole. a. Square blade shank, to be used with a wrench for large screws. b. Standard blade and tip for general use. c. Phillips screwdriver. d. Stubby screwdriver for tight spots. e. Offset type for use in awkward spots. f. Yankee (spiral ratchet) when driving a number of screws rapidly, e.g., opening and closing crate lids.

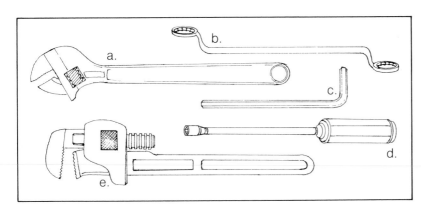

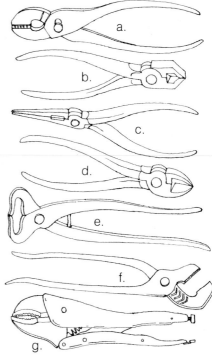

Figure 109 Wrenches

Wrenches come in a wide variety; the following are but a few that are useful in exhibition work. a. Adjustable wrench generally fits all nuts and bolt heads. b. Offset double-end box wrench has great strength and can be used in tight quarters. c. Allen wrench, also called a hex-key wrench, fits the hexagonal recesses in various Allen-type screws and set screws. d. Nut driver is used to fit hex nuts and works the same as a screwdriver. e. Stillson (pipe) wrench is used primarily for pipes.

Figure 110   Rulers, Squares, Levels and Markers

These aids will help to keep your lines straight and spaces equal. a. Steel tape rule—measures straight as well as round areas, is extremely flexible. For gallery use we recommend a 12′ rule as well as 50′. b. Folding wood rule—general measuring. c. Steel rule—accurate measuring during construction. d. Rafter square—general marking and aligning right angles. e. T-square—testing surfaces for squareness and marking right angle cuts. f. Combination square—testing for squareness and marking right angle cuts and 45° marks and cuts. g. T-bevel—measuring an angle and transferring it to another area or material. h. Levels—a check that the installation is straight. They come in wood or aluminum in lengths to suit various purposes; we recommend a 3′ carpenter's level (1) and a 1′ torpedo level (2), which can fit into areas others cannot. i. Carpenter's compass/divider—marking in pencil or inscribing on a flat surface for circular cuts. j. Marking gauge—drawing a parallel line on the edge of a board or panel before cutting. k. Trammel points—marking a large circle or curve with a constant radius. The trammel points are clamped onto a wood batten or metal rod. Chalk line (not illustrated)—marking a very long, straight line on a wall or floor. This is useful in lining up structures on the floor. Chalk a piece of string, have someone hold the string at point A, walk to point B, pull the string taut, lift it and let it snap back leaving a thin chalk line.

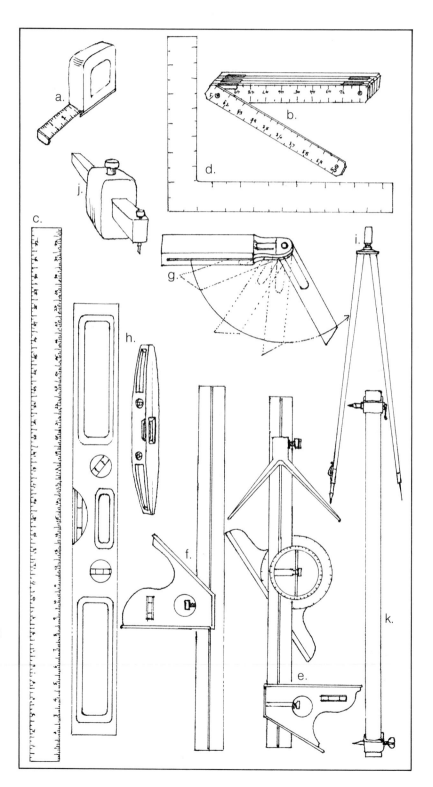

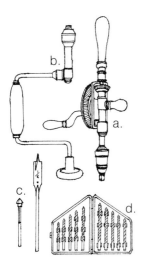

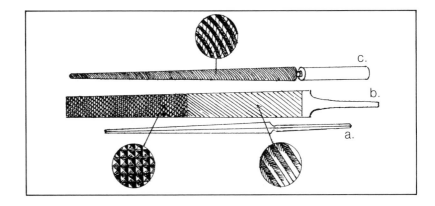

Figure 111   Hand Drills, Braces and Bits

a. Hand drill—an all-round drill used for drilling wood, metal or plastic with straight shank twist drills (d). (To start a hole in wood or soft plastic, use an awl to punch a small starter hole; with metal use a center punch.) b. Bit brace—drilling into wood, primarily. c. Drill bits—have a tapered shank with a variety of cutting edges especially for drilling larger holes up to three inches. One can also use a screwdriver bit in the brace, which is useful for hard-to-remove screws.

Figure 113   Chisels

These are used to chip away wood. They are struck by a mallet.

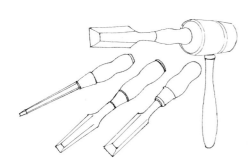

Figure 112   Files

Select the proper file for a specific job. For rapid strokes use a double cut file, applying heavy pressure. For a smoother finish use a finer, single cut file. Always clean them with a wire brush and store in protective sleeves to prevent dulling. a. Needle file—slender file with a knife cross section for delicate machine work. b. 4-in-hand rasp file—highly versatile; half of this file is rasp cut, half is file cut. c. Rattail file—a round, tapered file used to smooth out recesses or enlarge holes; very useful.

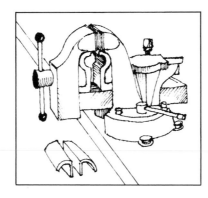

Figure 114   Vise

Mount a swivel-base bench vise on a tool cart or work table. For full-range use, use a bolt-mounted vise with a jaw width and opening of at least 3½″ and with replaceable jaws. This tool is an absolute must.

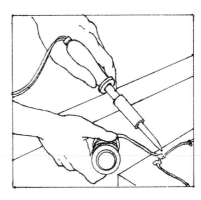

Figure 115   Soldering Gun

This is a handy tool to have when making wire armatures to hold display objects, soldering wire, making repairs in plastic objects and cutting openings in floor tiles. An electric soldering gun comes with changeable tips.

129

Figure 116   Clamps

Clamps are used when gluing. Which one to use depends on the size and shape of the glued material.

a. C-clamps—for heavy pressure required to glue two pieces together. Always insert "pads" of scrap wood between the jaw clamps and material for protection. Pads also help to distribute pressure uniformly. C-clamps come in sizes from one to eight inches (maximum opening of the jaws). Start with the 4″ C-clamp and buy at least four. Over the years you can add to the collection as needed by buying both smaller and larger jaw sizes.

b. Spring clamps—light duty work where heavy clamping pressure is not required. This kind is ideal for fast-setting glue work. As with all clamps, use a pad to protect the material. Spring clamps come in sizes from about four to eight inches in length with jaw openings of ¾-inch to three inches. Start with the 6″ spring clamp and buy eight.

c. Pipe clamps—cabinet and furniture work. In museums they are used to glue panels. We recommend using ¾″ pipe of 5′ and 9′ lengths. The jaw of the clamp assembly will screw onto one threaded end of the pipe for the fixed end while the other jaw assembly rides on the pipe with a wedge mechanism and clamping screw. You will need four clamp assemblies for each width of a panel; one clamp below and one above the work to prevent bending at one end, and another pair of clamps at the other end of the panel—one above and one below. For constructing a standard 4x8′ panel you need two sets of pipe lengths (four 5′ lengths and four 9′ lengths).

d. Web clamps—fiber bands with a locking device for gluing and clamping irregular shapes and drawing together several joints. They can be used for gluing frames and pedestals. The fiber band is looped around the work and pulled taut by the clamp body, which has a locking device tightened by a crank or ratchet. The band, either canvas or nylon webbing, is soft so that the work being clamped will not be marred. We recommend that you have at least two sets of web clamps in your tool collection.

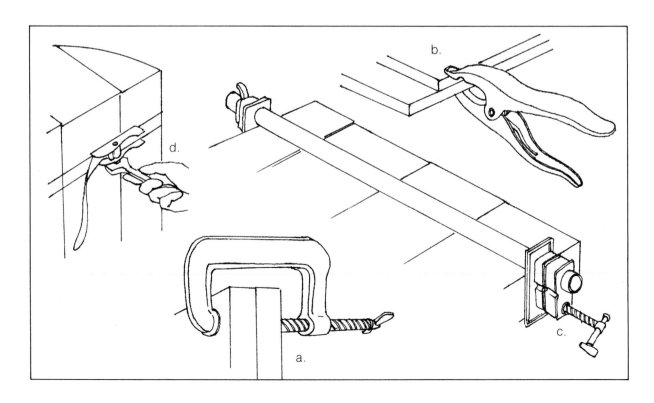

□ *Sandpaper and Coated Abrasives*

These papers smooth surfaces and remove imperfections. When sanding, use a sanding block to get an even finish. Sandpaper comes in the following grades:

1. Very fine—sanding between coats of paint, varnish or lacquer or to give an extra smooth finish before applying the first coat.
2. Fine—final sanding before applying a primer or sealer or to remove light rust and imperfections from metal.
3. Medium—removing rust stains and preparing walls for painting.

4. Coarse—sanding rough wood stock and smoothing deep scratches and imperfections.
5. Extra Coarse—removing heavy coats of paint and rust.

Many different kinds and grades of coated abrasives belong in your tool collection. Aluminum oxide paper is a fast cutting abrasive well suited for grinding and finishing extremely hard materials. Silicon carbide is much harder than aluminum oxide and is excellent for finishing hard plastics, glass and ceramics. It is also used for finishing brass, copper and aluminum. This abrasive can be used dry or wet.

Figure 117   Scissors

a. A good pair of paper scissors should have at least 4½″ blades. They should be used only to cut paper. b. Hawk-billed metal snip is a versatile heavy duty scissor for cutting sheet metal, vinyl tile and heavy cardboard.

Figure 118   Brushes

The brushes recommended here are for cleaning only. Buy quality animal hair brushes, the softer the better (animal hair is best for enamel or varnish). Buy a 1″, 2″ and 4″ brush.

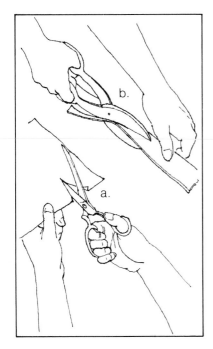

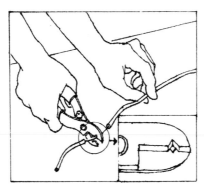

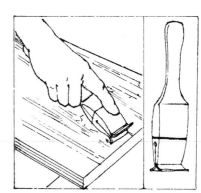

Figure 119   Wire Stripper

The multi-purpose wire stripper will strip, cut and crimp the ends of electric wire.

Figure 120   Scraper

A hook scraper will reduce a rough surface and can be used with paint or varnish remover. For finer surfaces, a putty knife will suffice.

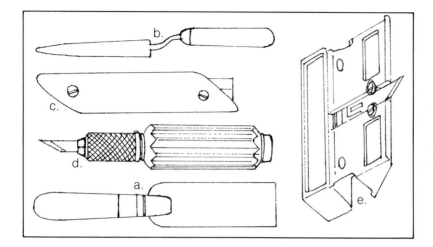

Figure 121   Heavy Duty Stapler

This tool is normally used for installing building insulation and can be found in a hardware or art supply store (artists use it to stretch canvas). It is useful in making fabric-wrapped panels or securing stretch fabrics over a frame.

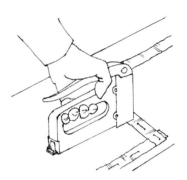

Figure 122   Knives

a. Putty knife—With a flexible stainless steel blade, this knife is used for applying and smoothing putty or spackle. It is also handy for filling, scraping and cleaning. b. Pallette knife—normally used by artists to mix pigments. We recommend you have one for fine work in filling cracks and nail holes in plaster walls. c. Mat knife—cuts heavy paper or paper mats. This has a heavy handle that takes single-edged razor blades (other types take special blades). d. X-acto knife—a commercially available model-maker's tool that accepts a number of interchangeable blades and used primarily for cutting paper, balsa wood and cardboard. It is handy during the exhibit installation for trimming labels and masking tape, and for cutting string, monofilament line and other light materials. e. Mat board cutter—a specially designed instrument for cutting mat boards. If you do a lot of graphic framing, it is invaluable. The cutting edge can be tapered to any angle.

Figure 123   Awl

The common awl is helpful in starting a hole for a nail or screw, lining up two pieces of metal before inserting a bolt, and punching holes in soft materials.

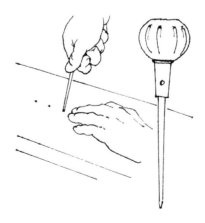

Figure 124   Wrecking Bar/ Crowbar

This tool is used to remove large nails or spikes (with the claw end), to pry open certain packing crates—by inserting one end of the bar under a heavy object and using a block of wood as a fulcrum—and to dismantle old exhibit panels and structures.

■ Power Tools

One or two heavy duty extension cords, at least 20 feet long, are necessary to use with the following power equipment. They should have male and female three-pronged plugs in order to properly ground the tools while in operation. Use a quad box (numerous outlets) to avoid repeated unplugging when operating several power tools.

Four Basic Power Tools

Figure 125   Electric Drill

An initial purchase should be a ⅜″ variable speed, reversible electric drill. This is a versatile tool that can drill wood, metal, plastic and concrete as well as perform other functions, such as disc sanding and grinding.

Some ⅜″ drills come with useful accessories, such as a stand on which to mount the drill horizontally for use as a grinder for sharpening tools and drill bits, and a vertical stand that converts the hand drill into a small drill press. Safety goggles must be worn when the drill is used with the two stands. The ⅜″ drill is equipped to handle a wide variety of drill bits (a), countersinks (b), cutters (c), grinders and discs (d) (for grinding and sanding) as well as paint stirrer (e), screwdriver attachment (f) and paint sprayer attachment (not illustrated).

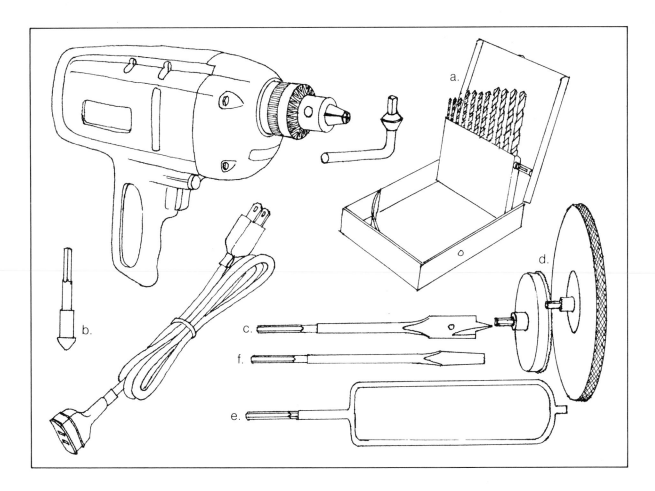

Figure 126   Saber Saw
(Portable Jigsaw)

A good saber saw will pay for itself in a very short time because
it is a versatile piece of equipment. Most saber saws will cut
through 2″ wood; they can make
straight or curved cuts in wood,
plywood, homosote, laminates
and light metal. A good one will
rip a long piece of wood (with a
rap fence), crosscut, bevel, miter
and start a cut in the middle of a
panel. With a carbide-tipped
blade, the saber saw will also
cut glass and tile. Blades for
other cutting work include
metal-cutting blade for iron, steel
and brass (a), coarse-toothed
blade for thick wood (b), fine-
toothed blade for hardwood and
plastic (c), knife blade for
linoleum, rubber and leather (d)
and taper-ground blade for a
smooth edge (e).

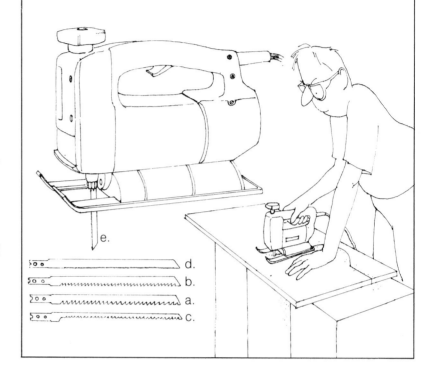

**Figure 127   Electric "Orbital"
Sander**

This is used primarily as a
"finishing" sander since it moves
in a small circular motion. Some
orbital sanders can be switched
from the circular motion to
straight line sanding by moving
a lever. This sander has a removable pad over which
sandpaper is stretched. Worn-out
sandpaper will not cut, so check
its condition from time to time.
The orbital sander can also be
used to sand filled nail or screw
holes in plaster and, with a wool
pad, to polish Plexiglas.

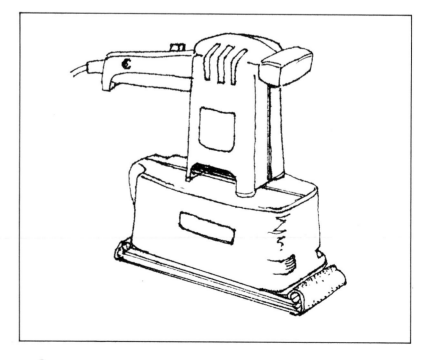

Figure 128   Circular Power Saw

The portable saw that you select should be capable of cutting a 2x4 at a 45° angle and have a minimum blade size of seven inches in diameter. Other things to consider are whether the saw can make shallow cuts by having a depth adjustment and whether it has an angle adjustment (for cutting miters and bevels) and a ripping fence (which will guide the saw for a straight cut to a prescribed width). For safety purposes it should have a spring-actuated blade guard that retracts when the blade is cutting and then snaps back when the cut is complete. Different blades will do different work.

When not in use saw blades should be kept in their protective sleeves. When used heavily the blades should be sharpened. If you get saw burns or if the blade binds, it is probably dull.

a. Combination crosscut and rip blade is used for thick or thin softwoods and hardwoods (with or across the grain), as well as plywood and hardboard. This is the best all-round blade.
b. Crosscut blade has fine teeth and cuts across the grain smoothly. It is also excellent for a smooth cut on plywood, hardboard and veneers. This blade should not be used for ripping. c. Rip blade has large teeth and is used for heavy cutting with the grain. A guide bat-

ten (length of wood clamped to the wood being cut) or a rip fence should be used for a more accurate cut. d. Abrasive blades of various kinds are designed for specific materials to be cut, such as masonry, metal, and some plastics. Buy the blade to suit the material.

Other blades not illustrated are: hollow ground blade, which gives the smoothest cut but requires continual sharpening (it cuts hard or soft materials, thick or thin, with minimal sanding required) and special carbide-tipped blade used for cutting Plexiglas. This blade must be treated carefully, kept sharp and used only for Plexiglas.

■ **Other Power Tools**

A fully equipped workshop should include the following power tools:

1. 8″ circular table saw
2. Drill press *(bench mounted)*
3. Router *(portable)*
4. Combination belt and disk sander *(on its own table)*
5. Grinder *(bench mounted)*
6. Jointer *(on its own table)*

■ **Fasteners**

□ *Nailing Tips*

- Use a nail three times longer than the thickness of the piece of wood through which it passes.

- When toenailing, offset opposing nails to pass each other.

- Drive nails at angles for a better grip; this is called dovetail nailing.

- Avoid nailing into the same grain line as this will probably split the wood.

- When nailing into hardwood, drill a pilot hole slightly smaller than the nail diameter.

- Use a heavy block of wood against the free side of a piece of unsupported work when you nail into it, to prevent bouncing.

- For blind nailing, chisel up a wood sliver and drive the nail into the recess, being careful not to break the sliver. Then glue the sliver back into position after the nail head has been countersunk with a nail set (this takes practice).

- To drive small nails or brads, use a thin piece of cardboard as a holder with a razor cut to the nail; drive the nail in halfway and pull the cardboard away, thereby protecting your fingers.

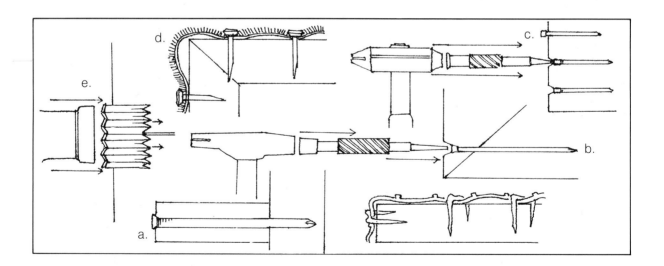

Figure 129 Nails

a. Common nail—general purpose for heavy duty work; the large head will not pull through.
b. Finishing nail—trim and cabinetwork where nailheads must be concealed. The finishing nail is sunk into the wood with a nail set and then filled over.
c. Common brads—the smallest of finishing nails, for fine work like attaching molding, frame construction, etc. This nail is also sunk and then filled.
d. Tacks—fasten carpet or fabric to wood. e. Corrugated fastener—miter joints, such as large frames or pedestal fabrication. f. Staples—not to be confused with the staple used in a staple gun. The (nail) staple is heavier and is used to hold wire or electric cable.

□ *Choosing the Right Screw*

Screws are used for greater holding power and when parts may have to be separated. There are two types—wood screws and metal screws—and two types of screw heads—the common slotted and the crossed slot known as the Phillips. Another distinction in wood screw heads is whether the head is oval, round or flat in profile.

Select a screw for maximum holding power without splitting the wood. The length should be chosen so that two-thirds of it fits into the material. Before starting the job, experiment with some scrap lumber.

To insert a screw, make a pilot hole with an awl for smaller screws and with a drill and bit for larger ones. The drill bit should be at least two sizes smaller than the screw-thread diameter. When working with hardwood, or with exceptionally large diameter screws in wood subject to splitting, drill both a pilot hole and clearance hole for the screw shank one-third the length of the screw. When fastening screws in a new piece, wax or soap the threads.

Most screws used in exhibit installation are wood screws. On the rare occasion when you work with metal, use metal screws. The most common metal screw is the Panhead, with a pointed end. Because the metal screw has more threads per inch than the wood screw, it can sometimes be used as a high strength fastener for plywood and hardwood. When fastening into a plaster wall, the metal screw should be used with a plastic molly.

When fastening with a screw, locate and mark the screw position with a pencil. With a scrap piece of wood underneath, drill a hole through the first piece of wood. This hole, the clearance hole, should be large enough to pass the shank of the screw. If a flathead screw is to be used, then for a clean and flush finish countersink the clearance hole to match the screw head: the fit should be flush. After that, position the drilled piece of wood in the exact location where it is to be fastened on the base piece of wood. Be careful not to move the wood as you mark the base piece of wood with an awl or a nail. You should now drill the pilot hole in the base piece of wood to a depth

half the length of the screw. Make the pilot hole diameter two times smaller than the threaded part of the screw so that the screw thread can bite into the wood. Then wax or soap the screw and drive it into place with a screwdriver (remembering to use a screwdriver that fits the head slot), drawing the two pieces of wood tightly together.

□ *Nuts and Bolts*

These fasteners are used for strength and dependability. Nuts and bolts generally connect large panels together, a large object to a panel, or an exhibit case to a panel. When using nuts and bolts to fasten elements, the bolt must pass through both pieces. Using washers at either end of the bolt will add to the grip of the nut and bolt without excessive marring of the surface finish.

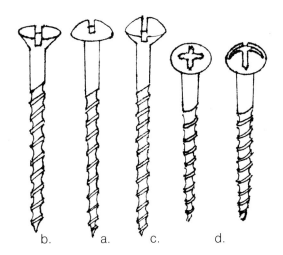

b.   a.   c.   d.

Figure 130

Screws

a. Roundheads—for work likely to be disassembled (the slot is deeper) and where thin materials such as sheet metal are fastened to wood. b. Flatheads—the screwhead is flush to the surface. surface. c. Ovalheads—for countersinking. d. Phillips head—cross slotted screw to minimize screwdriver slippage. The cross slots are available in most head types; however, use with a Phillips screwdriver.

Figure 131 Bolts

a. Machine bolt is made with square or hex head forms and with square or hex head nuts; fine or coarse threads are available.

b. Carriage bolt has a shoulder with either a flat topped head or a round head. The nut is generally square. The shoulder keeps the bolt from turning when nut is tightened so that the shoulder will dig into the work.

c. The stove bolt is a general utility bolt and can be tightened with a screwdriver while the nut is held with a wrench.

d. The turnbuckle is made of two screw eyes and a steel sleeve; one half of the sleeve and one screw eye have a right-handed thread and the other half of the sleeve and the screw eye have a left-handed thread. The turnbuckle is used with cable or heavy wire to tighten up tension support, i.e., to straighten out warped panels or tighten wires in tension to eliminate sagging. Note: for safety, always seek assistance before using turnbuckles.

e. Toggle bolts and molly bolts are used for fastening to hollow walls.

f. Eye bolts, J bolts and U bolts are special holders used when these shapes serve a particular purpose. For example, U bolts can hold pipe tubing or wooden poles and the eye bolt can be securely attached to suspended element when a normal screw might have the tendency to "pull out."

g. Hanger bolt or screw has one end threaded like a wood screw that can be driven into wood, while the other end has a machine thread that will accept a nut or a special fitting.

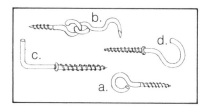

Figure 132 Screw Hooks

The ordinary screw hook is a simple hook on which to hang things. The screw eye (a), through which picture wire can be strung, is sometimes attached to frames. It is also used as a light anchor; it can suspend small or light elements, and wire strung horizontally for supporting elements. For the latter, the gauge of the shank size is usually heavier. Other types of screw hooks are the eye and ring (b), the square bend screw hook (c), and the cup hook (d).

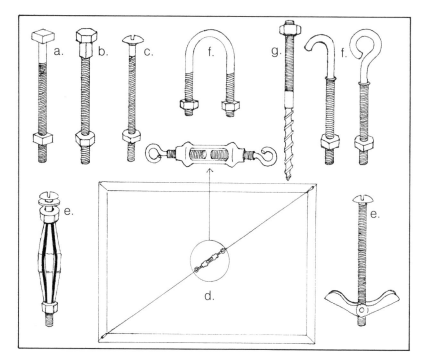

Figure 133 Strap Hangers

Also called mirror hangers, this is a handy device for suspending frames and small panels. The curved hook part of the hanger rotates easily and takes up very little space. This type of hanger can be left on a frame when not on display because there are no sharp edges or corners to cause damage.

Figure 134   Special Fittings

A number of fittings, plates and brackets have excellent applications in exhibit fabrication.
a. Keyhole plates—hang exhibit cases on walls or panels. They can be mounted either on a wooden strip on the wall or attached to the case. The keyhole plate hangs on a round head screw projecting from the opposite surface. b. Cam-action locking device—draws two units together, such as two flat panels. c. Corner brace—cast or stamped metal right-angle connection much stronger than the standard angle iron. Holes in the corner brace are usually countersunk to accept flat head screws. d. Threaded inserts—connect two elements that will be disassembled. The insert has an outer thread for installing into one piece of wood and an inner machine thread to take a bolt that goes through the second piece of wood. e. Clips—fasten a horizontal panel to a vertical panel. f. Leg plates—attached to the bottom of a case or riser; legs with hanger bolts or screws threaded into them are then screwed into the leg plates.

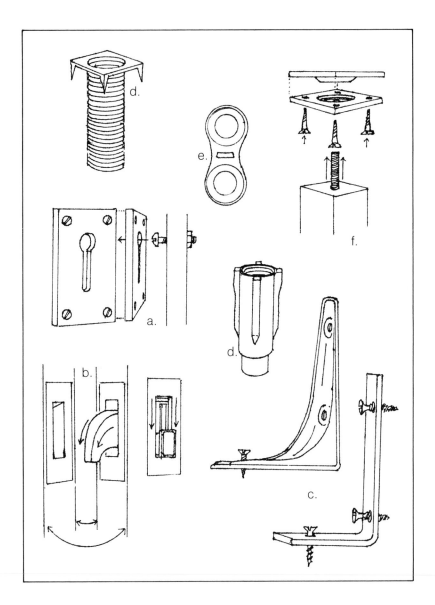

■ Adhesives

Before selecting an adhesive you must consider the characteristics of the different types available and how you are going to use it. Some adhesives resist moisture (in a humid environment); others can set in a cool environment. Some require a long setting time or clamping. For best results, follow the manufacturer's directions. If you are unsure which to use, ask at the hardware store.

Listed here are nine types of adhesives and their uses, along with sample brand names. Most generic glues (glues of the same type but sold under different brand names) work in the same manner, though may be less expensive than others. Shop around.

□ PVA Adhesives
These popular "white glues" come ready mixed and can be purchased in hardware, variety, and

139

drug stores. Properties of these Polyvinyl Resin adhesives make them well suited for most interior wood-working projects. They dry clear, with a strong bond (although work should be clamped, if possible). Since this glue is water soluble, the excess can be cleaned off with a damp cloth or sponge. Note that adhesives will not resist high stress or dampness.

Brand Names: Elmer's Glue-All; DuPont White Glue; Sears White Glue; Franklin Concrete Adhesive White Glue; Duralite White Glue; Evertite White Glue; and Tite Bond White Glue.

□ *Contact Cements*
These are used to bond laminates such as Formica or Micarta to plywood. This type of adhesive is also excellent for gluing plastic foam, hardboard, masonite and metal to wood. (It should not be used for normal wood gluing.) You must apply the adhesive to both work surfaces evenly and allow it to dry. They must be accurately positioned before touch since up to 75 percent of the full bonding strength is achieved upon contact. Some craftspersons do what is called "slip sheeting": to do this, place a large sheet of brown kraft paper between the two glued surfaces just shy of one end, align the work and press the two flush pieces together at that point. Then slowly remove (slip) the brown paper while continuing to press the glued surfaces together. Remove excess glue with a special solvent or with nail polish remover.

Brand Names: Devco Rubber; Pliobond; Sears Miracle Pliobond; Craftsman Contact Cement; Weldwood Contact Cement; Juro Contact Cement; Woolworth's Contact Cement; and Duralite Contact Cement.

□ *Rubber Base Cements*
These non-structural adhesives can be used to bond wood to concrete, paper to paper, paper to wallboard, and rubber to rubber. Use a special solvent or nail polish remover to clean off excess adhesive. This is not to be used on exhibit objects, prints, posters, photographs and like items.

Brand Names: Gripit; Ozite AP880; Scotch Grip; Miracle Adhesive; Black Magic; High Tak Super Adhesive No. 975; and Poly-Chemical's Strip-Cure. Note: These are not the standard rubber cements used only for adhering paper to paper.

□ *Epoxy Adhesives*
Almost all materials can be glued with epoxy adhesives. However, because they are very costly and somewhat cumbersome for large projects, their use should be limited to general repairs such as those on glass and china and forming strong metal-to-metal bonds. Epoxies usually come in two containers—one a resin and one a hardener—to be mixed according to directions. Epoxies are usually slow curing.

Brand Names: Helor Quik-Set; Kling Enterprises Epoxy; 5-Minute Epoxy; Epoxy 1177; Ruscoe Epoxy; Elmer's Epoxy; Devcon Clear Epoxy; and Wilhold Epoxy.

□ *Plastic Cements*
These are for general repair, form strong bonds and have high resistance to moisture. They are used also in model making. Plastic cements can be used to glue glass, wood, plastic and china. Work should be clamped, if possible, or positioned in a sandbox so that the two pieces being glued (the mend) are balanced one over the other. Excess glue should be removed with acetone.

Brand Names: Duco Cement; Liquid Solder; Scotch Super-Strength Adhesive; Wilhold China and Glass Cement; Devco Plastic Mender; and Weldit Cement.

□ *Latex Base*
These adhesives, which come in tubes and tins, are used in gluing carpeting, fabrics, cardboard and paper. They dry quickly and form strong flexible bonds. The bonds can be washed in hot water without any effect on their grip. Dry cleaning or the use of solvent cleaners should be avoided. Excess adhesive should be wiped off with a damp rag before the adhesive sets. Dried adhesive can be removed with lighter fluid.

Brand Names: Devcon Patch; Sears Stitchless Mender; Durelite Formula 55; and Franklin Indoor-Outdoor Carpet Adhesive.

□ *Mastic*
These are adhesives used to bond ceiling tiles, floor tiles, plywood wall paneling or similar building materials. There are two distinct types of mastic adhesives—one a water soluble latex and the other a rubber resin type in a petrochemical solvent. Both types bond well to concrete, hardboard, asphalt, ceramic tiles, leather and textiles. Surplus adhesive can be removed with a damp rag, but once hardened require a petrochemical solvent.

Brand Names: Webtex 200 Acoustical Adhesive; Franklin Construction Adhesive; and Ruscoe Pan-L-Bond.

□ *Resorcinol and Formaldehyde*
Both of these adhesives are excellent for bonding wood when exceptional structural strength is required. As resorcinol is mixed with a resin, it should be used where dampness or high humidity is present. The formaldehyde adhesives, through extremely strong, are not recommended for damp conditions because they are mixed with water.

■ Painting Aids

□ *Brushes and Rollers*
Painting is relatively easy; techniques are not complicated and the tools simple to use. Paint brushes should be of the finest quality since they hold more paint and provide a smoother stroke. Test them for bounce; they should feel springy and elastic when pressed gently on any flat surface.

   Good brushes are expensive, so take care of them. Always clean a brush right after painting; do not wait until the next day. For oil-base or alkyd paints use turpentine followed by paint thinner; finish with soap and lukewarm water. For latex or water-base paints simply wash in lukewarm water, using soap if necessary. Brushes used with shellac, lacquer or alcohol stains

Both formaldehyde and resorcinol require clamping from three to ten hours. Neither adhesive should be used in a work area where the temperature is below 70 degrees.

Brand Names: Craftsman Plastic Resin Glue; Weldwood Plastic Resin Glue; Sears Waterproof Resorcinol Glue; and U.S. Plywood Waterproof Resorcinol Glue.

□ *Gums and Paste*
This broad class of adhesives includes flour pastes, animal glues, starch and dextrine adhesives and rubber cements. These glues are used solely for adhering paper, cardboard and leather. With the exception of the rubber cements, excess glue can be removed or cleaned with water. Excess rubber cement should be removed with a rubber cement pickup (a square of crepe rubber).

Brand Names: Carter's Liquid Paste: Carter's Mucilage; Carter's Rubber Cement; Higgins Vegetable Glue; and Le Page's Paper Cement. Note: adhesives having a petrochemical base are extremely flammable so care should be taken when they are used. Open them in a well ventilated space because their fumes can be harmful.

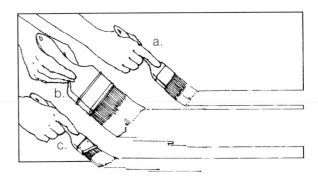

Figure 135   Brushes

A good assortment of brushes includes at least (a) two 1½" brushes, (b) two 4" brushes, and (c) one beveled sash and trim brush.

should be cleaned first in alcohol or lacquer thinner, then soap and lukewarm water. After washing, comb the brushes to straighten out the inner bristles. For storage, wrap them in heavy paper or aluminum foil.

Rollers are one of the greatest painting aids yet devised. To clean, roll off excess paint on newspaper and remove cover from the handle. Clean as instructed for brushes, and store dry covers in aluminum foil.

For roller painting, you will need at least two roller paint trays and a collection of covers—lamb's wool for general wall use with latex or oil-base paints; mohair for extremely smooth surfaces such as exhibit panels, and perhaps some long-nap covers for ceiling or rough surfaces.

Other equipment needed for painting is a drop cloth, ladder, scraper, putty knife, crack and nail hole filler (spackle) and sandpaper.

Figure 136 Brush Pads

An alternative to brushes and rollers are brush pads. These are less expensive than rollers, but the results are not as good. For a quick job that will not bear close inspection the brush pad is all right. You might experiment and see how it works for you.

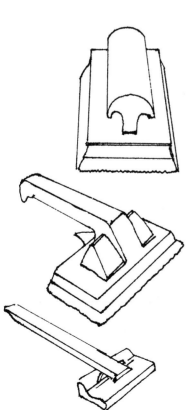

Figure 137 Rollers

These come in different sizes and shapes, with varying handle lengths or extensions, each tailored to a specific task. Shown are (a) 9″ surface roller for large areas, (b) trim roller for small areas, (c) V-shaped roller for corners, and (d) cone-shaped roller for corners.

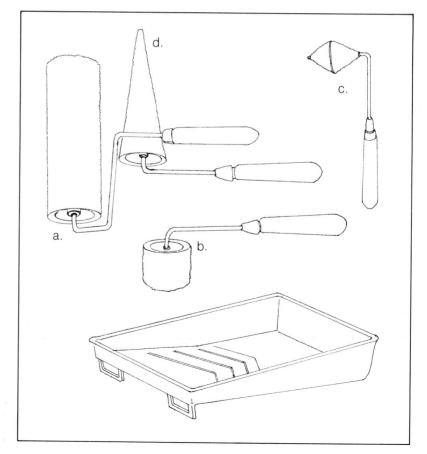

■ Graphic Tools

For preparation of scale drawings and model making, certain graphics tools will expedite the work.

- A 32″ x 42″ drawing board or a drafting table
- A T-square
- A 30°/60° plastic triangle
- A 45°/90° plastic triangle
- or a medium sized adjustable triangle
- An architect's scale *(ruler)*
- A set of drafting pencils
- A roll or pad of graph paper
- A roll of yellow tissue *(for overlays)*
- A metal straight edge *(36″)*
- An X-Acto knife with extra blades
- An erasing shield
- A collection of erasers *(pink, art gum and kneaded)*
- A bottle of rubber cement
- Rubber cement pickup
- A roll of ½″ masking tape
- A quality compass
- Tweezers
- Paper scissors
- A 36″ square paper cutter *(if your budget permits)*
- A 36″ wide dry-mounting press *(if your budget permits)*
- A flat file to store paper and drawings *(if your budget permits)*
- A set of PMS color swatches
- A Color Aid swatch book
- A desk lamp
- A desk brush
- Studio felt markers in various colors
- A 20-foot/metric measuring tape □

Chapter 11

Raw Materials

11

Raw Materials

■ Wood

The material you will use most frequently is
wood. Of all woods, pine (a softwood) is the most
economical and readily available. Hardwoods—
walnut, oak, teak, birch or mahogany—are preferred for exterior finishes because of their surface properties. These are used for molding,
framing, edging and cabinetwork. However, the
cost of hardwood lumber is probably beyond your
budget. You would do better to buy plywood with
a hardwood veneer and hardwood strips for edging and other details.

For framing, where the wood is not seen, the
least expensive pine is more than adequate; we
recommend D grade, numbers 1 or 2. Where the
wood shows but will be finished with stain or
paint, use a better quality such as B or C grades,
numbers 1 or 2.

Lumber is ordered by thickness, width and
length. Do not be confused when you measure a
piece, since all standard sizes are a few fractions
of an inch less. For example, a standard 2x4 refers to the lumber's *nominal* size, i.e., its original
rough sawed size, whereas the *actual* size is
1½"x3½".

The length of standard lumber starts at 8-foot
lengths and increases by 2-foot increments. Much
of the softwood lumber available today has rough

and often split ends; the split or crack might run
from three to nine inches into the board's grain.
Allow for this by ordering five to ten percent
more than you actually need.

Go to the yard yourself and check each piece
for warping, too many knots or loose ends. Many
softwoods have hard, brown pockets (knots) that
give off a sticky liquid. Before starting work,
clean these with turpentine, then shellac-seal
them. Loose knots should be white-glued, put
back in place and also shellacked.

Standard Sizes of Lumber

Nominal size (in inches)	Actual size (in inches)
1 x 2	¾ x 1½
1 x 3	¾ x 2½
1 x 4	¾ x 3½
1 x 5	¾ x 4½
1 x 6	¾ x 5½
1 x 8	¾ x 7¼
1 x 10	¾ x 9¼
1 x 12	¾ x 11¼
2 x 2	1½ x 1½
2 x 3	1½ x 2½
2 x 4	10½ x 3½
2 x 6	1½ x 5½
2 x 8	1½ x 7¼
2 x 10	1½ x 9¼
2 x 12	1½ x 11¼
3 x 4	2½ x 3½
4 x 4	3½ x 3½
4 x 6	3½ x 5½
6 x 6	5½ x 5½
8 x 8	7½ x 7½

■ Panel Materials

□ *Plywood*

A wide variety of plywood is available for both
interior and exterior use. Grades range from A
(smooth and paintable) to D (filled areas,
knotholes and splits). Group numbers run from
group 1, the strongest, to group 5, the weakest.
One side may be finished, both sides finished,

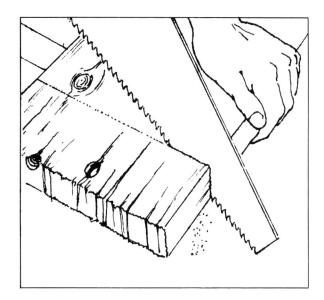

Figure 138   Squaring the End

Buy lumber a little longer than needed. Do the final cutting yourself (instead of paying the yard a cutting fee) to make sure the end cut is made at right angles.

hardwood exterior and softwood interior, hardwood throughout, and softwood throughout. Plywood comes in thicknesses ranging from ¼ inch to ¾ inch. Though generally sold in 4x8′ sheets, some grades and finishes come in 10′ and 12′ lengths. Large lumberyards sometimes stock, or else can order, non-standard sizes and thicknesses.

Duraply (a trade name) has a paper surface and comes in standard sizes and thicknesses. It is popular with many museums, in that it is inexpensive, can be easily painted, used for cut-out letters and for standard exhibit panels.

Where the plywood will not show, we recommend an A grade interior fir plywood, ⅜″ thick for general work. Use the ½″ or ¾″ for bases and platform fabrication.

Plywood can be mortised (a cutout recess),

dovetailed (notched), mitered (end grain cut on a diagonal) and generally worked in the same manner as solid wood, if it is thick enough.

Cutting Plywood: Use a fine-toothed saw. When sawing across the grain, score (cut with a sharp knife) the cut line. Be sure to score both sides of the plywood sheet in order to prevent splintering. When using a circular saw or a radial arm saw, turn the good side face up. When cutting with a portable power saw, turn the good side face down. If the plywood has two good surfaces, score both sides or apply paper masking tape along the cutlines; remove the tape by pulling it off away from the cut, avoiding splintering.

Screwing into Plywood: Always drill a pilot hole in plywood when using screws. Screws fastened to the face of plywood hold more securely than ones fastened in the edges. On a soft plywood, it may be necessary to use screw washers to prevent the screws from sinking too far into the wood.

Gluing Plywood: Use coarse sandpaper to roughen the surfaces. While the glue is setting, apply pressure with clamps, remembering to use scrap lumber between the gripping portion of the clamps and the wood surface. Should some of the plywood veneer lift up, glue and clamp the loosened area with a wood block and clamp.

☐ *Hardboard*

Hardboard, such as Masonite, is a versatile material ideally suited for panel fabrication. Uncut factory sheets, in 4′ widths and in standard lengths of 8′, 10′ and 12′, are true and square cornered for easy modular construction. Hardboard thicknesses are ⅛″, 3/16″ and ¼″, though thicker sheets may be ordered. This material is quite heavy so where weight could be a problem use ⅛″ birch plywood instead.

Hardwood comes in two types—tempered and untempered. The tempered is more dense (thus heavier) and quite hard, a result of having been treated with oils and resins. This treatment also makes it more resistant to moisture.

Hardboard is made smooth on one side (S1S)   147

or smooth on two sides (S2S). Standard wood-working tools can be used to cut and shape this material.

Cutting Hardboard: Always use a fine-toothed saw and cut on the face side. Score the cutting line with a sharp knife to minimize possible chipping. Since hardboard is thin and can break or tear easily if roughly handled, support the sheet at both ends. A batten (a long piece of straight wood) clamped along the cutting line will prevent the saw's veering from the line or ''jumping'' and damaging the surface. For cutting a curved line use the narrowest blade on a portable power saber saw. To get the sharpest curves, use a hand coping saw. Always clamp the work to prevent chattering or possible jumping. If you are cutting a curve on a ⅛″ hardboard sheet, clamp the hardboard to a piece of plywood in a number of places to give it support.

Gluing Hardboard: All woodworking adhesives work well with untempered hardboard. When gluing the smooth face of the hardboard, roughen the surface with coarse sandpaper. When working with tempered hardboard, sand the area and use epoxy glues.

Fitting Hardboard: Always drive screws or brads *through* the hardboard into the material below, never the other way around. If nailing, use special hardboard brads that have very small heads.

Handling Hardboard: Hardboard panels should be stored flat to protect edges and corners that

break or dent easily. Avoid damaging or roughening the smooth surface of hardboard, as sanding will not restore the original smoothness. Nor can you hide scratches with paint.

□ *Chip Board*
This material, also called particle board, is made from sawdust and wood chips mixed with a resin and pressed into sheets. Less expensive than plywood and somewhat heavier, it is ideal for construction that does not show, such as bases and pedestals covered with cloth. For maximum

Figure 139   Hardboard Panel

Hardboard is usually framed when used as a panel, although it sometimes is suspended by chain or wire. The corners are rounded because they break easily. Drill two holes and reinforce them with grommets (metal eyelets). Paint the hardboard and wet-mount graphics.

holding power, brads, nails and screws should be driven through the chip board and into the material. Gluing and clamping are recommended for a more secure bond.

If handled carefully, chip board edges can be mitered, but you may have to use a wood filler to patch chipped areas, then sand and finish. Chip board is not normally used as a finished material. Two types are available—an interior and exterior grade, in three-layer or extruded form. We recommend the three-layer, the strongest. It comes in several thicknesses.

□ *Upson Board*
This material is made from plant fibers or wood pulp formed into light, stiff, inexpensive panels. Upson board is found in a range of thicknesses ⅛" and larger in interior and exterior grades. It comes in 4' widths and can be purchased in 6', 8' and 12' lengths. The ⅛" board is flexible enough to bend into a 12" diameter, so that circular pedestals can be fabricated if properly framed with fir plywood. Upson board takes paint well. While it is easily cut with a saber saw and other saws, it leaves a somewhat ragged edge that must be sanded. Upson board does not take to nails because of its softness; it should be glued and clamped. Good as it is for temporary structures (panels, pedestals) it is not recommended for permanent structures or traveling exhibitions because of its softness. It will not take abuse. Its "one time" use is justified by the price.

□ *Homosote and Cellotex*
Both of these "soft" fiberboards, primarily an insulation, can be effectively used as panel material. Their soft surfaces are easy to "pin into." Both should be stored flat since the corners can break off if not handled carefully. Use flat head nails to fasten one of these boards to a wood frame, since finishing nails or brads will not hold. Homosote and Cellotex boards come 4'x8'; in ½" to 1" thicknesses. Odd sizes may be specially ordered if the quantity merits it. You can easily wrap these panels with cloth or burlap by stapling on the back surface and then mounting the covered panel in a heavy wood frame.

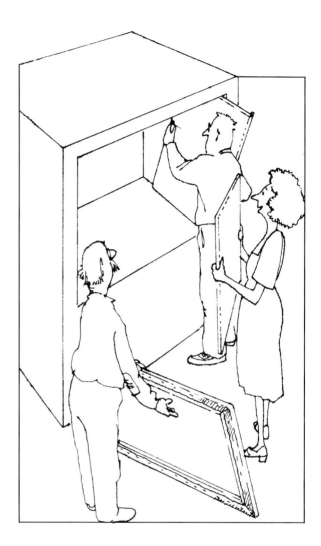

Figure 140

Covered Panel

When designing the exhibit, consider using cloth as a background for the objects. Collect several fabric swatches and experiment with different cloth-wrapped panels in a mockup case.

□ *Laminates*
For a long-lasting surface or one bound to receive much abuse, a plastic laminate bonded on plywood or chip board works well. A variety of wood grains and plain colors in matte or gloss finishes is available. For use on horizontal surfaces, a ¹⁄₁₆" laminate is recommended; for vertical surfaces, a 1/32". Standard sheets measure

from 2′x5′ up to 5′x12′. It is advisable to back all laminate-covered surfaces (to prevent absorption of moisture, which may warp the board), but it is not necessary when the board is to be firmly fastened to a frame. Contact cement is the best adhesive to mount the laminate to raw plywood. Instructions on how to cut, install and trim plastic laminates can be obtained from your lumber yard.

□ *Foamcore*
One of the lightest sheet materials available is foamcore. Obtainable from art supply stores in 40″x60″ sheets and some hardware stores and manufacturers in 4′x8′ sheets, it comes in thicknesses of ³⁄₁₆″, ¼″ and ½″. Cut with a mat knife or fine saw blade.

Foamcore is backed on both sides with white or brown paper. It is good for wet-mounting photographs or labels. However, you will have to "counter mount" with kraft paper on the reverse side to eliminate warping. Foamcore is ideal for cutouts such as maps, figures or shapes used as background in a case.

□ *Cardboard*
Box manufacturers sell various gauges of cardboard and it can be used in the exhibit in many ways—as backing for photographs (photomurals) or graphics, and structurally for case furniture. Corrugated cardboard, obtainable from display houses or point of purchase suppliers, lends textural effects as case backing or pedestal wrapping. Corrugated cardboard comes in different colors, but we recommend painting it yourself since the standard colors seem to fade quickly. Also useful is a vinyl-impregnated cardboard.

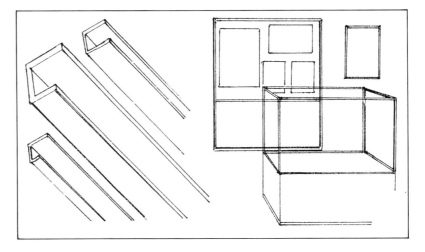

Figure 141 Metal Dividers

Expanded metal sheets and perforated metal sheets of many patterns and thicknesses can be framed in wood and used as dividers for a certain amount of transparency. Cut with a hacksaw or special metal-cutting blade on a saber saw. Remove burrs with a file.

Figure 142 Metal Frames

Iron and aluminum angle irons or channel stock can be used to frame large panels and exhibit cases. Smaller angles can frame glazed graphics, paintings and photographs. Buy them at lumberyards and hardware stores.

□ *Cloth and Vinyls*

Many elegant effects can be achieved by wrapping a panel, pedestals or risers with cloth or vinyl sheeting. Everything from burlap, felt and unbleached muslin to silk or velour can add richness to your installation that mere paint cannot accomplish. Cloth and vinyls offer not only rich textural variety but also a wide range of colors. To wrap a panel, measure the surfaces to be covered and prepare a schedule (list each surface separately with its measurements). For example, for a 3'x6' panel, you need a piece of cloth at least 3'6" x 6'6" to cover the face and fold around the back for stapling.

■ **Metal**

Besides nails, screws and bolts and other connectors, metal can be used in a variety of ways. Sheet metal, various wires and bar and rod stock of steel or brass are used to form armatures and cradling devices to hold objects on display. Metal sheets can serve as dividers (Figure 141) and angle irons as frames (Figure 142).

Metal foils and some mylar foils can line case interiors and cover small pedestals and risers. However, the subject matter must be compatible with this "slick" treatment such as, perhaps, contemporary jewelry or science and technology. The use of foils is risky because foils are reflective. Lighting and object placement should be worked out first in a scale model, then a full scale mockup. Foils are sold by art supply stores and some wallpaper distributors.

□ *Pipes and Tubing*

Since so many standard pipe fittings and aluminum tubings are available from a hardware or plumbing supply store, there is no difficulty in obtaining parts for a structural system. Prepare scale drawings indicating lengths of pipe as well as the number and types of connectors. You may even have to build a small model out of balsa wood in order to visualize the three-dimensional configurations.

To guarantee proper fit, have the supplier cut and thread the ends of the pipe. Several pipe

wrenches will be useful to assemble and disassemble the structure.

Aluminum tubing can be sheared with a "pipe and tubing" cutter or a hacksaw with a blade that has 24 or 32 teeth per inch. Burrs are removed with a file.

Continued insertion and removal of connectors in aluminum tubing will in time stretch its interior, causing a loose fit of the connectors.

■ **Glass**

Even though glass is heavier and more difficult to work, not to mention breakable, many museum professionals prefer glass over plastic. It is cheaper, easier to clean, and free from the electrostatic problems and softness of plastics.

Most glass used for exhibit cases is ¼" plate glass; for framing graphics, photographs, drawings and watercolors—1/16".

To prepare for cutting, measure all four sides because the frame or opening may not be exactly square. If two parallel sides differ, choose the smaller dimension. Before cutting case glass, deduct ¼" from the total of each of the two dimensions to allow for expansion and contraction. For frame glass, deduct ⅛" from each dimension. Glass may crack with changes in temperature, especially if used in a metal frame or in metal mullions with no room for it to expand.

Cutting glass efficiently is a matter of experience. It is a good idea to practice on scrap glass. You will need a glass cutter and a straightedge.

■ **Plastic**

Most traveling exhibitions use sheet plastic (Plexiglas or Perspex) in frames because of its strength and flexibility. There is little breakage unless the plastic has been cut "too tight" and causes pressure within a frame that could result in a crack if the frame were dropped or bent.

Exhibit cases are most likely made of sheet plastic. Here too, rough treatment may cause cracks. It is a good idea to be ready to make repairs and cut new pieces. You may also wish to learn how to make plastic cases and cut plastic for your own frames.

151

Figure 143   Aluminum Tubing

Tubing used in folding lawn chair frames lends itself nicely to a structure. Since aluminum is lighter than iron pipe, order a 1″ outer diameter with a relatively thick wall for strength. Connectors fit the tube's inside dimensions.

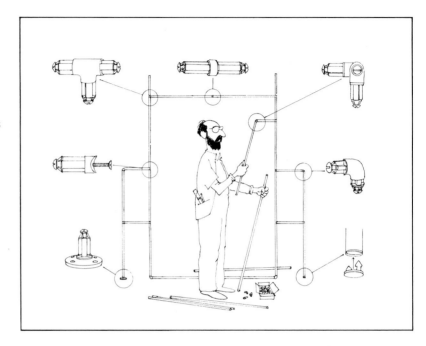

Figure 144   Iron Pipes

Many exhibition designers use ordinary galvanized plumber's pipe as a structural system with clean, contemporary style. The pipe should be 1″ in diameter.

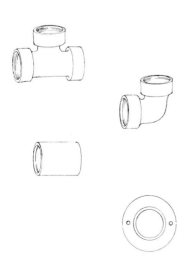

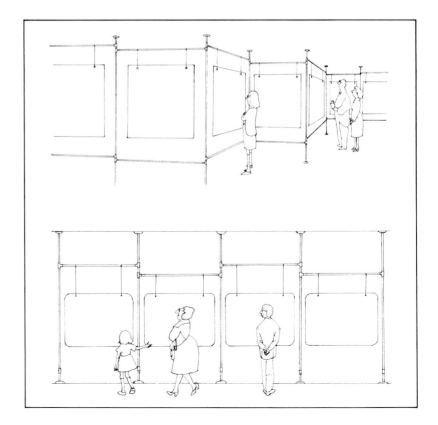

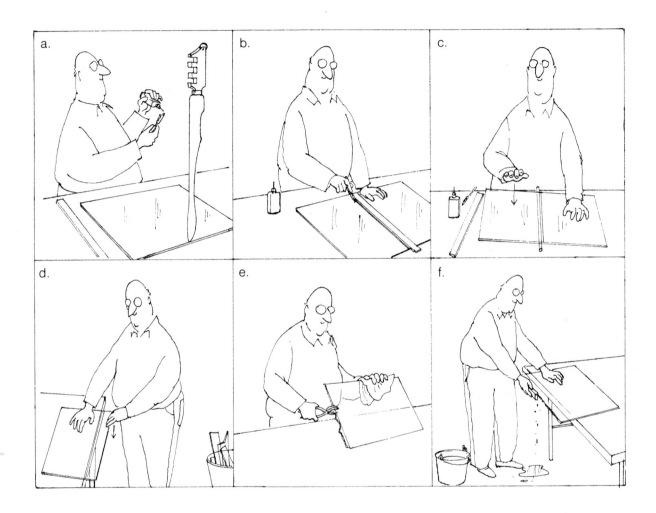

Figure 145   The Process of Cutting Glass

a.   The cutting wheel should be oiled with a thin machine oil or kerosene.

b.   Holding the flat part of the cutter with your index finger, score the glass along the straightedge in one smooth, firm stroke. Rescoring a missed spot is a bad practice since the glass will probably shatter irregularly at that point.

c.   After scoring, place a long wooden dowel under the cut line, raising the glass about ½". Press on each side to snap the glass.

d.   If the cut line is close to the edge of the glass, place the sheet over a table edge and gently tap the underside to open up an inch or so of the score line. Then grasp the glass on each side of the line and snap off the waste. Press downward and away from the score line.

e.   If the waste piece does not snap off evenly, the remainder can be cut off with a wide nosed lineman's pliers or slip-joint pliers. Grip the glass with the pliers and, with a downward motion, trim off the waste

f.   Raw edges can be smoothed with oilstone dipped in water.

To counter the effect of plastic's static electricity, use an anti-static cleaner recommended by the plastic manufacturer. Never use tape on Plexiglas, or detergent for cleaning.

Plastic sheets, rods and blocks can be cut and drilled with regular woodworking tools. Keep a set of blades (fine-toothed) for your jigsaw, band saw and circular saw for use only on plastic. Sharp blades will prevent burrs and small nicks.

All plastic comes with a protective "cover paper" on both sides that peels off when the edges are cut and smoothed. Since plastic's relatively soft surface scratches easily, leave on the cover paper until it is installed.

Plastic sheeting also comes with ultraviolet (UV) filtering properties. Rohm & Haas, makers of Plexiglas, has a clear sheeting UF1 up to 48″ × 96″, and UF III in the same size but with a slightly yellow tint and better UV absorbing capabilities. UFI and UF III can be worked like ordinary Plexiglas.

ICI, the British chemical firm that makes Perspex, also has two UV filtering products—VA Clear, an acrylic sheet that absorbs 98 percent of UV radiaton, and VE Clear that absorbs 99 percent of UV radiation but has a slightly yellow color.

Both manufacturers' products afford excellent protection against sunlight and fluorescent light that give off dangerous UV radiation. The ⅛″ plastic sheeting can be cut for use in frames to protect drawings and prints, while the thicker ¼″ is appropriate for exhibit cases.

Cutting Plastic: Scribe a deep line through the paper into the plastic along a straightedge (which should be clamped at each end of the sheet). Place a wooden dowel beneath the cut, lengthwise, and press down on each side of the line to break the plastic. A jigsaw, with a batten clamped at each end of the sheet, will also cut plastic, but be sure the blade clears the work table. A fine-toothed, hollow ground blade can be used on a circular saw.

For curved shapes, mark a cutting line on the cover paper and use a jigsaw or stationary band saw. Cut slowly to avoid burrs. If a power saw

begins to bind while cutting plastic or if the plastic heats up, the blade needs either sharpening or replacing.

The cut edge should be smoothed with a medium, then fine-grade wet or dry sandpaper or aluminum oxide paper, or even silicon carbide paper. Wrap the abrasive paper around a sanding block. For a transparent edge, sand with an extra-fine paper and follow with a buffing wheel mounted on a ¼″ electric hand drill. The plastic manufacturer also sells buffing compounds—like rouge—that make the task much easier.

Drilling Plastic: Drill in the same manner as wood. Use a hand or electric drill or a drill press. Work over a wood base at a low speed.

Gluing Plastic: Use adhesives recommended by the manufacturer. Here again we suggest that you practice with scrap pieces. Plastic can be unglued with a solvent (recommended by the manufacturer) and reused if still reasonably clear and unscratched. Minor blemishes can be buffed with a very fine abrasive and a buffing wheel to look almost like new.

Plastic sheets, adhesives, solvents, polishing compounds and cleaning/anti-static liquid are stocked by most lumberyards.

■ Paint

Latex and *alkyd* are the paints most often used for exhibitions. Latex (semi-gloss and flat) thins with water, spreads easily, dries in an hour, has little or no odor and can be cleaned off brushes and rollers with only soap and water. Alkyd paint (gloss enamel, semi-gloss and flat) has more covering capability than latex. It thins with paint thinner or turpentine, dries in an hour, has little odor. Brushes and rollers used with alkyd paints must be cleaned with paint thinner or turpentine, then washed with soap and warm water. When using either paint on a raw surface, give it a coat of primer or sealer first.

Acrylic and *epoxy* are used on concrete and wood floors. The finish is glossy, hard-wearing and easy to clean. Directions on the can will tell you

Figure 146   New Look for Old Textures

For unusual effects, materials like sand, gravel and ground cork can be spread on the floor and curbed with wood or even brick. Before trying this kind of display, however, check with the organizer to make sure the objects can be safely set on a pebble surface. Ceramics and crafts are considered "safe."

how to prepare the floor and how to clean rollers.

Lacquers are glossy, semi-gloss or matte (not truly flat). They are usually sprayed and have a very hard finish that is easy to clean. Lacquers are used by most display houses (firms that fabricate exhibits) for panels, exhibit cases, pedestals and exhibit case furniture. Unless you have in-house spraying facilities —a spray booth or fire-proof and explosion-proof room—do not attempt to spray with lacquer. Have it done by a display house or even an auto repair shop.

Spray cans of enamels, lacquers and acrylics are invaluable for covering small objects like panels, pedestals, case backs and furniture. Aerosol spray paint comes in many colors. Spraying should be done in a well ventilated room. Since most aerosol paints are flammable, do not spray near an open flame. Mask the area around the object with tape and newspaper. You might experiment on a piece of cardboard to find the best spraying distance. When you have finished clear the nozzle by turning the can upside down and spraying until the paint stops coming out. Store the cans in a cool place, far away from hot-water and heating pipes.

Before You Paint . . .

- remove protruding nails, picture hangers, tape. (Tape adhesive dissolves in thinner or lighter fluid.)

- fill in holes and cracks with spackle, then sand and dust surfaces with a dry mop.

- clean finger marks and other greasy stains with a strong detergent and water.

- sand spackled areas and paint with primer or sealer.

- prime or seal raw wallboard, chip board, plywood and fiberboard.

- have a sturdy ladder with folding platform to hold the paint can.

- keep visitors out of the area, since footsteps raise dust particles that adhere to freshly painted surfaces.

Every paint job will go faster if you follow a logical sequence: do ceilings first, then walls, trim (floor molding, doors and door molding), windows and floor last.

Paint exhibit parts elsewhere if possible. If not, spread a large drop cloth on the floor and rest the pieces on wooden horses or blocks.

■ Other Materials

A neutral background that is not distracting can show off a wide variety of objects to their best advantage. On the other hand, a background can be specifically chosen to emphasize quality or function of the artifacts on display. For example, cork insulation panels, weathered boards from houses and barns, or even a wall of old bricks and mortar may be considered an integral part of the display and not just a gimmick. If using ''old'' or ''used'' materials, make sure that they are free from insects and loose dirt.

Look around a hardware store and lumberyard for different substances with interesting textures, like cork, stone and brick veneer, mirror tiles and floor tiles of ceramic, vinyl, rubber and wood. All of these can be mounted on plywood panels and used as background. □

Chapter 12

Sources

The following suppliers and manufacturers can be contacted for catalogues and technical reports, most of them free of charge. The selection of suppliers and manufacturers is that of the author and is not intended as a commercial endorsement.

Materials, Tools and Equipment

Plywood and Panels
Technical reports and data from:

Plywood panels

The American Plywood Association
119 A Street
Tacoma, WA 98401

Wood panels

Hardwood Plywood
Manufacturers Assoc.
P.O. Box 6246
Arlington, VA 22206
703-671-6262

Weldwood Paneling
Champion Building Products
One Landmark Square
Stamford, CT 06921

Melamine component panels and high-pressure laminates

Formica Corporation
Wayne, NJ 07470
201-831-1234

Wood panels

Georgia-Pacific
900 S.W. Fifth Avenue
Portland, OR 97204

Hard board

Masonite Corporations
29 North Wacker Drive
Chicago, IL 60606

Vinyl-faced gypsum panels

United States Gypsum
101 South Wacker Drive
Chicago, IL 60606

Note: All telephone numbers should be confirmed with the information operator in their respective cities or regions.

Building board, panels, moldings, adhesives

Homasote Company
West Trenton, NJ 08628

Styrofoam and plastic

Central Plastics
527 South Wells Street
Chicago, IL 60607

Styro Materials
2519 Walnut Street
Denver, CO 80202

Arthur Brown & Brother, Inc.
2 West 46th Street
New York, NY 10036
212-575-5555

Cutout Letters

Letters Unlimited
272 High Street
Closter, NJ 07624
201-768-5844

Scott Plastics Co.
P.O. Box 2958
Sarasota, FL 33578
813-355-5171

Lake Shore Markers
Erie, PA 16512
800-458-0463 (toll free)

Miscellaneous Metal

Perforated metal and expanded metal

McNichols Co.
4889 East 154th Street
Cleveland, OH 44128
Toll free 800-321-1240

Aluminum gratings and other metal products

Reliance Steel Products Co.
3700 Walnut Street
McKeesport, PA 15134
412-461-3616
or 751-1000

Perforated metal, plastic and hardboard

National Perforating Corp.
Parker Street
Clinton, MA 01510
617-368-8761

Perforated metals

Harrington & King
Perforating Co., Inc.
East Crescent Ave. at Arrow Road
Ramsey, NJ 07446
201-825-2380

Hardware

Catalogue available (most complete source)

McMaster-Carr Supply Company
P.O. Box 4355
Chicago, IL 60680
312-833-0300

Catalogue available

Brookstone Company
Peterborough, NH 03458

Allcraft Tool & Supply Co., Inc.
15 West 29th Street
New York, NY 10036

X-Acto knifes, model making tools, frame making equipment

X-Acto
45-35 Van Dam Street
Long Island City, NY 11101
(Dept. TAL-8)

Screws, nuts, bolts, anchors, self-locking sockets, cotter pins, milled studs, etc. (catalogue available)

United States Fastener Corporation
8100 Schoolcraft Avenue
Detroit, MI 48238
313-491-8860

Latches and fasteners (catalogue available)

South Co., Inc.
Concordville, PA 19331
215-459-4000

*Case hardware, display lighting
(catalogue available)*

Garcy Corporation
2501 North Elston Avenue
Chicago, IL 60647

Case hardware (catalogue available)

Selby Furniture Hardware Company
15-19 East 22 St.
New York, NY 10010
212-OR 3-4097

*Rolled metal shapes
(catalogue available)*

Teledyne Metal Forming
Elkhart, IN 46514

*Metal corner clips (catalogue and
free booklet
available on case and furniture
construction)*

Fitch Creations, Inc.
Box 111
Chapel Hill, NC 27514

Fabrics, banners

Banners Unlimited, Inc.
5 Copley Road
Larchmont, NY 10538
914-834-3999

Vinyl wall covering

Glidden Coatings & Resins
Cleveland, OH 44115

Borden
Columbus Coated Fabrics
Columbus, OH 43216

B.F. Goodrich Company
General Products Division
500 S. Main Street
Akron, OH 44313

Flannel, jute wall covering

Specialty Jute Products &
Development, Inc.
Southwest Park
P.O. Box 337
Fairforest, SC 29336
803-576-0965

Miscellaneous product information

Display World
407 Gilbert Avenue
Cincinnati, OH 45202

Art Supplies (mail orders)

Arthur Brown & Bro., Inc.
2 West 46th Street
New York, NY 10036
212-575-5555

A.I. Friedman, Inc.
25 West 45th Street
New York, NY 10036
212-245-6600

Audio-Visual Equipment

Catalogue for a minimal price

*"The Audio-Visual Equipment
Directory: A Guide to Current
Models of Audio-Visual Equipment"*

National Audio-Visual
Association, Inc.
3150 Spring Street
Fairfax, VA 22030
703-273-7200

General sources and catalogues of
films, slides, pictures and other
learning materials are listed in
"Sources of Audio Visual
Materials" in the *Guide to Historic
Preservation, Historical Agencies,
and Museum Practices: A Selected
Bibilography*. New York State
Historical Association,
Cooperstown, Rev. ed. 1975.

Lighting Systems

*Track lighting, low voltage fixtures,
plus a full range of other
exhibit lighting*

Lighting Services, Inc.
150 East 58th Street
New York, NY 10022
212-838-8633

*For low emission ultra-violet
fluorescent lamps*

Verilux, Inc.
35 Mason Street
Greenwich, CT 06830

*Track lighting, low voltage
fixtures, plus a full range of
other exhibit lighting*

Edison Price Incorporated
409 East 60th Street
New York, NY 10022
212-838-5212

*Write for nearest showrooms
and regional representatives*

Executive Offices Lightolier, Inc.
346 Claremont Avenue
Jersey City, NJ 07305

Track lighting, low voltage fixtures

Lightcraft of California
1600 W. Slauson Avenue
Los Angeles, CA 90047

*Track lighting, write for nearest
showrooms and
regional representatives*

General Offices
Prescolite A.V.S.
Industries Company
1251 Doolittle Drive
San Leandro, CA 94577
414-562-3500

*Track lighting, write for
nearest regional representatives*

Halo Lighting Division
McGraw-Edison Company
400 Busse Road
Elk Grove Village, IL 60007
312-956-8400

Swivel-socket and çlamp-on lamps

Swivelier Company
33 Route 304
Nanuet, NY 10954

Structural Exhibit Systems

System Abstracta

Abstracta Structures, Inc.
38 W. 39th Street
New York, NY 10018
212-944-2244

Alka Structures

Alka Structures, Inc.
41-51 28th Street
Long Island City, NY 11101
212-784-1040

Apton System

Apton System-Intra Systems Corp.
14700 Doolittle Drive
San Leandro, CA 94577
415-895-8570

Bigscreen System

Giltspur Exposystems
3225 South Western Avenue
Chicago, IL 60608
312-376-3000
Toll free 800-621-6028

System Connectra

System Connectra
Technical Exhibits Corp.
6155 South Oak Park Avenue
Chicago, IL 60638
312-586-6500

System 8

System 8
Gingerbread Displays, Inc.
1051 Clinton Street
Buffalo, NY 14240

Gallery Panel System

Gallery Panel System
Dimensional Communications, Inc.
200 LeGrand Avenue
Northvale, NJ 07647
201-767-1500

Klem Fastener System

Klem Fastener System
Youngstown Design Center
435 Main Street
Youngstown, NY 14174
716-745-3662

Multiscreen System

Giltspur Exposystems
3225 South Western Avenue
Chicago, IL 60608
312-376-3000
Toll free 800-621-6028

Opto System

Opto, Incorporated
162 Northfield Road
Northfield, IL 60093
312-441-7570

*Sho-Wall System and
Timber Toppers*

Sho-Wall System
The Brewster Corporation
Old Saybrook, CT 06475
203-388-4441

Unistrut System

Unistrut Corporation
35005 Michigan Avenue West
Wayne, MI 48184
313-721-4040

The following are other industrial
structural systems adaptable for
exhibition usage which are not included in our analysis on page 57:

*Meroform (a space frame system)
and Telespar Tubing*

Unistrut Corporation
35005 Michigan Avenue West
Wayne, MI 48184
313-721-4040

*Channel System and
Space Frame System*

Power-Strut Division
Van Huffel Tube Corporation
Warren, OH 44481
216-372-8111

Space Frame System

Triodetic Structures Group
Butler Manufacturing Company
P.O. Box 917
Kansas City, MO 64141

Space Frame System

P.G. Structures, Inc.
39 East 20th Street
New York, NY 10003
212-475-1460

Tubing, connectors, bars, and shapes

Julius Blum & Co., Inc.
P.O. Box 292
Carlstadt, NJ 07072
201-438-4600

Barriers and Traffic Control
Devices and Poster Stands

*Posts, ropes as well as tubing,
signs and frames*

Lawrence Metal Products, Inc.
P.O. Box 400-M Dept. SW
Bay Shore, NY 11706
516-666-0300

Inframes
Giltspur Exposystems
3225 South Western Avenue
Chicago, IL 60608
312-376-3000
Toll free 800-621-6028

*Poster stands: check
Structural Exhibit Systems
for addresses of:*

Abstracta Systems
Alka Structures
Apton System
System Connectra
System 8
Sho-Wall System
Unistrut System

Archival Preservation and Presentation

Write for catalogue

The Hollinger Corporation
P.O. Box 6185
3810 South Four Mile Run Drive
Arlington, VA 22206
703-671-6600

Process Materials Corporation
329 Veterans Boulevard
Carlstadt, NJ 07072
201-935-2900

Light Impressions
Box 3012
Rochester, NY 14614
716-271-8960

Len Hartnett Archival Products
300 N. Quidnessett Road
North Kingstown, RI 02852
401-884-1480

Energy Conservation and Preservation of Cultural Properties

A wide range of free literature

Energy Information Clearing House
Box 241
New York, NY 10024

Keeper, Department of Conservation
Victoria and Albert Museum
London, S.W. 7, England

Security Consultants

*Directory of U.S. Security
Consultants,* Law Enforcement
Standards Program, Law
Enforcement Assistance
Administration, National Institute
of Law Enforcement and Criminal
Justice; U.S. Department of
Justice, Washington, D.C. 20530

The directory has alphabetical
entries, includes description of
services, summary of experience,
list of publications. Alphabetical,
geographical and subject indexes.

The directory can be ordered from
the Superintendent of Documents,
U.S. Government Printing Office,
Washington, D.C. 20402, Stock No.
LESPRPT-0309.00

Other references provided by

The American Society for
Industrial Security
Museum Security Committee
2000 K Street, NW
Washington, DC 20006

The Handicapped

Free

The National Arts & the
Handicapped Information Service
ARTS
Box 2040, Grand Central Station
New York, New York 10017

-Architectural Accessibility
-New Programs and Facilities
-Technical Assistance, Information
 Centers & Consultants
-Annotated Bibliography of
 Publications & Media
-Arts for the Blind and Visually
 Impaired
-Arts Education for Disabled Students
"Museums and Handicapped
 Students: Guidelines for
 Educators"

*A free publication of the
Smithsonian Institution listing
sources and bibliography,
write to:*

Coordinator, Programs for
the Handicapped, Room 3566,
National Air and Space Museum,
Smithsonian Institution,
Washington, D.C. 20560

*A comprehensive survey of
accessibility*

*Arts and the Handicapped: An
Issue of Access,* Education
Facilities Laboratory (EFL), 850
Third Avenue, New York, NY
10022

Copies available for sale

Program assistance

Museum Access Planning Sources,
M*A*P*S
Skye Pictures, Inc.
2225 Floyd Avenue
Richmond, VA 23220

Publications

Association for the Education of
the Physically Handicapped
919 Walnut Street
Philadelphia, PA 19001

National Association of the Deaf
814 Thayer Avenue
Silver Spring, MD 20910

Convention of American
Instructors of the Deaf
5034 Wisconsin Avenue, N.W.
Washington, D.C. 20016

*For the disabled, resource persons,
program information*

Closer Look
Box 1492
Washington, D.C. 20013

Resource persons, literature, training, etc.

Rehabilitation Institute of Chicago
345 East Superior Street
Chicago, IL 60611

Research, publications, aids, etc.

American Foundation for the Blind
15 West 16th Street
New York, NY 10011

Resource persons, literature

National Federation of the Blind
218 Randolf Hotel Building
Des Moines, IA 50309

National Traveling Exhibition Organizations*

Non-profit traveling exhibition services

American Federation of Arts
41 East 65th Street
New York, NY 10021
212-988-7700

American Institute of Graphic Arts
1059 Third Avenue
New York, NY 10021
212-752-0815

Association of Science-
Technology Centers
Traveling Exhibits Service
1016 Sixteenth Street, N.W.
Washington, DC 20036
202-452-0655

Independent Curators, Inc.
1740 N Street, N.W.
Washington, D.C. 20036
202-872-8200

International Exhibitions Foundation
1729 H Street, N.W., Suite 310
Washington, D.C. 20006
202-298-7010

International Museum of Photography
at the George Eastman House
900 East Avenue
Rochester, NY 14607
716-271-3361

Museum of Modern Art
National Program of
Circulating Exhibitions
11 West 53rd Street
New York, NY 10019
212-956-2635
956-5903

Oak Ridge Associated Universities
Museum Division, Traveling Programs
P.O. Box 117
Oak Ridge, TN 37830
615-483-8411

Pratt Graphics Center
160 Lexington Avenue
New York, NY 10016
212-685-3169

Smithsonian Institution
Traveling Exhibition Service
A & I Building, Room 2170
Washington, D.C. 20560
202-357-3168

Visual Studies Workshop, Inc.
Four Elton Street
Rochester, NY 14607
716-454-6556

Western Association of Art Museums
Department of Circulating Exhibitions
Mills College
P.O. Box 9989
Oakland, CA 94613
415-568-2775

* There are also corporate, national association and state traveling exhibitions. For further information on state and regional sources contact your state's arts and humanities councils.

Chapter 13

Bibliography

General

Books

Adams, T.R. *The Museum and Popular Culture*. New York: American Association for Adult Education, 1939.

Kepes, Gyorgy, ed. *The Visual Arts Today*. Middletown, Conn.: Wesleyan University Press, 1960.

Lewis, Ralph H. *Manual for Museums*. Washington, D.C.: National Park Service, 1976.

Museums USA. National Endowment for the Arts, 1974. Washington, D.C.: U.S. Government Printing Office, 1974. Stock Number 036-000-00024.

Parr, A.E. *Mostly About Museums*. New York: The American Museum of Natural History, 1959.

Rea, Paul Marshall. *The Museum and the Community*. Lancaster, Pa.: The Science Press, 1932.

Reiss, Alvin H. *The Arts Management Handbook*. Law-Arts Publishers, Inc., 1970.

Smithsonian Institution Conference on Museums and Education, University of Vermont, 1966. *Museum and Education Papers*. Ed. by Eric Larrabee. Washington, D.C.: Smithsonian Institution Press, 1968.

Taylor, Francis Henry. *Babel's Tower*. New York: Columbia University Press, 1945.

Tilden, Freeman. *Interpreting Our Heritage: Principles and Practices for Visitor Services in Parks, Museums and Historic Places*. Rev. ed. Chapel Hill: University of North Carolina Press, 1967.

Wittlin, Alma S. *Museums: In Search of a Usable Future*. Cambridge, Massachusetts: MIT Press, 1970.

Periodicals

Display World (a monthly publication) Display Publishing Co., 407 Gilbert Avenue, Cincinnati, Ohio 45202.

History News can be ordered from American Association for State and Local History, 1315 Eighth Avenue South, Nashville, Tennessee 37203.

Other national and international organizations with publications:

The American Association of Museums and (ICOM) International Council of Museums, 1055 Thomas Jefferson St., N.W., Washington, D.C. 20007.

The (British) Museums Association, 87 Charlotte Street, London, W1, England.

Canadian Museums Association, 331 Cooper Street, Suite 400, Ottawa, Ontario K2P 0G5, Canada.

International Institute for Conservation of Historic and Artistic Works (IIC), 176 Old Brampton Road, London SW 5, England.

National Park Service, Department of the Interior, Washington, D.C. 20240.

National Trust for Historic Preservation (NTHP), 1785 Mass. Ave., N.W. Washington, D.C. 20036.

United Nations Educational, Scientific and Cultural Organization (UNESCO), 1 rue Miollis, Paris XVᵉ, France; and UNESCO Publications Center, 801 Third Avenue, New York, New York 10022.

Bibliographies on All Aspects of Museology

Borhegyi, Stephan F., and Elba A. Dodson. *A Bibliography of Museums and Museum Work, 1900-1960*. Milwaukee, Wis.: Milwaukee Public Museum Publications in Museology, No. 1, 1960.

Borhegyi, Stephen F., and Irene A. Hanson. *A Bibliography of Museums and Museum Work, Supplementary Volume 1960-61*. Milwaukee, Wis.: Milwaukee Public Museum Publications in Museology, No. 3, 1961.

Rath, Jr., Frederick L., and Marilyn Rogers O'Connell. *Guide to Historic Preservation, Historical Agencies, and Museum Practices: A Selective Bibliography*. Rev. ed. Cooperstown, N.Y.: New York State Historical Association, 1975.

Planning and Designing Exhibits

Adams, P.R. "The Exhibition," *The Organization of Museums: Practical Advice*. Paris: UNESCO, 1960.

Birren, Faber. *Color for Interiors: Historical and Modern*. New York: Whitney Library of Design, 1963.

Black, Misha (ed.). *Exhibition Design.* London: Architectural Press, 1950.

Brawne, Michael. *The New Museum.* New York: Frederick A. Praeger, 1965.

Carmel, James H. *Exhibition Techniques, Traveling and Temporary.* New York: Reinhold Publishing Co., 1962.

"Effective Exhibits—A Search for New Guidelines," *Museum News,* 46:5 (January, 1968).

Garland, Ken. *Graphics Handbook.* New York: Reinhold Publishing Co., 1966.

Gardner, J., and C. Heller. *Exhibition and Display.* London: William Clowes and Sons, Ltd., 1960.

Gutmann, Robert. *Exhibition Stands.* London: Alex Tiranti, Ltd., 1962.

Lawless, Benjamin W. "Museum Installations of a Semi-Permanent Nature." *Curator,* Vol. I, No. 1. New York: American Museum of Natural History, 1958.

Nelson, George (ed). *Display.* New York: Whitney Library of Design, 1953.

Temporary and Traveling Exhibitions. Paris: UNESCO, 1963.

U.S. National Park Service, "Museum Planning, The Exhibit Room and Its Equipment, Museum Exhibits," *Field Manual for Museums.* Washington, D.C.: U.S. Government Printing Office, 1941.

Graphics and Design Periodicals

Communications Arts. Published by Coyne & Blanchard, Inc., P.O. Box 10300, 200 California Avenue, Palo Alto, California, 94303.

Graphis. Published by Walter Herdeg, Graphis Press, P.O. Box 320, New York, New York 10005.

New Graphic Design. Published by Hans Neuburg, Zurich, Switzerland.

Print. Published by RC Publications, Inc., 527 Madison Avenue, New York, New York 10022.

Domus. Via Monte de Pieta 15, 20121 Milan, Italy.

Progressive Architecture. Published by Reinhold Publishing Co., 600 Summer Street, Stamford, Connecticut 06904.

Multi Media/Audio-Visual

Eboch, Sidney C. *Operating Audio-Visual Equipment.* San Francisco, Calif.: Chandler Publishing Company, 1960.

Kissiloff, William. "How to Use Mixed Media in Exhibits," *Curator,* Vol. XII, No. 2, The American Museum of Natural History, 1969.

Mahaffey, Ben D. *Relative Effectiveness and Visitor Preference of Three Audio-Visual Media for Interpretation of an Historic Area.* College Station, Texas: Texas A & M University, 1969.

Multi Media Periodicals

Audiovisual Instruction. (monthly, September to June, subscription) Department of Audiovisual Instruction, National Education Association, 1201 16th Street, N.W., Washington, D.C. 20006.

Educational Screen and Audio-Visual Guide. (monthly subscription) 434 South Wabash Avenue, Chicago, Illinois 60605.

Museum Education

Newsom, Barbara Y., and Adele Z. Silver, eds. *The Art Museum as Educator.* Berkeley: University of California Press, 1978.

Public Relations

Cutlip, Scott M. *A Public Relations Bibliography,* 2nd ed. Madison, Wis.: University of Wisconsin Press, 1965.

Getting in Ink and On the Air: A Publicity Handbook. Boston, Mass.: Metropolitan Cultural Alliance, Inc., 1973.

Getting the Word Out—and the Message Across: a Publicity Handbook. Wilmington, Delaware: The Delaware State Arts Council, 1977.

Golden, Hal, and Kitty Hanson. *How to Plan, Produce and Publicize Special Events.* Dobbs Ferry, N.Y.: Oceana Publications, 1960.

The Public Relations Journal. Published by Public Relations Society of America, 375 Park Avenue, New York, New York 10022.

Tools and Fabrication, General

Briggs, Rose T. "Displaying Your Costumes: Some Effective Techniques," *History News* 21:1 (January 1966) Technical Leaflet No. 33.

Carmel, James H. *Exhibition Techniques, Traveling and Temporary*. New York: Reinhold Publishing Co., 1962.

Daniels, George. *The Awful Handyman's Book*. New York: Cornerstone Library, distributed by Simon & Schuster, 1969.

Denver, Edward F. "Silk Screen Printing and Museum Exhibits," *Curator*, Vol. VII, No. 3, American Museum of National History, 1964.

Getteus, R.J., and G.L. Stout. *Painting Materials–A Short Encyclopedia*. Rev. ed. New York: Dover Publications, 1966.

Gilbertson, Henry Walter. *Educational Exhibits, How to Prepare and Use Them, A Manual for Extension Workers*. U.S. Department of Agriculture Handbook No. 32. Washington, D.C.: U.S. Government Printing Office, 1951.

Gladstone, Bernard. *Hints and Tips for the Handyman*. Rev. ed. New York: Cornerstone Library, distributed by Simon & Schuster, 1967.

Henderson, Stuart M.K., and Helen Kapp. "Special Exhibitions." *Handbook for Museum Curators* F2. London: The (British) Museums Association, 1959.

Hirsch, Richard. "Exhibits and Installations: An Outline Guide," *History News* 19:7 (May 1964) Technical Leaflet No. 20.

Jones, William K. "Preparing Exhibits: The Use of Plexiglass," *History News* 24:2 (February 1969) Technical Leaflet No. 49.

MacBeth, James A., and Alfred C. Strohleim. "The Use of Adhesives in Museums," *Museum News* 43:9 (May 1965), Technical Supplement No. 7.

Moseley, Spencer, et al. *Crafts Design: An Illustrated Guide*. Belmont, Cal.: Wadsworth Publishers, 1962.

Muscutt, H.C. *Display Technique*. New York: Taplinger Publishing Co., 1964.

"Museum Exhibition Techniques," *Midwest Museums Quarterly* 14:3 (July 1954), entire issue.

Neal, Arminta. *Help for the Small Museum*. Boulder, Col.: Pruett Press, 1969.

"Preparing Your Exhibits: Methods, Materials & Bibliography," rev. ed., *History News* 24:10 (October 1969) Technical Leaflet No. 4

Reader's Digest: Complete Do-It-Yourself Manual. The Reader's Digest Association, Pleasantville, New York, 1973.

Temporary and Traveling Exhibitions. Paris: UNESCO, 1963.

Labels and Typography

Bahr, Leonard F. *ATA Advertising Production Handbook*. Third Edition. New York: Advertising Typographers Association of America, Inc., 1963.

Bloch, Milton. "Labels, Legends and Legibility," *Museum News*, 47:3 (November 1968), pp. 13-17.

Christensen, Erwin O. "Labels for Masterpieces," *Museum News*, 43:9 (May 1965), pp. 29-31.

Garland, Ken. *Graphics Handbook*. New York: Reinhold Publishing Co., 1966.

Luckiesh, M. and A.A. Eastmann. "Footcandles for Critical Seeing," *Illuminating Engineering*, Vol. 41 (1946), pp. 826-46.

Moss, F.K. *Reading as a Visual Task*. New York: D. van Nostrand Co., Inc., 1942.

North, F.J. "Museum Labels," *Handbook for Museum Curators*, B. 3. London: British Museums Association, 1957.

Paterson, D.G., and M.A. Tinker. *How to Make Type Readable*. New York; Harper Brothers, 1940.

Williams, Luther A. "Labels: Writing, Design and Preparation," *Curator Journal*, Vol. 3, No. 1 (1960), pp. 26-42.

Lighting

Brommelle, N.S., and J.B. Harris. "Museum Lighting, Part 1," *Museums Journal* 61:3 (December 1961), pp. 169-177; "Part 2—Artificial Lighting and Museum Display," *Museums Journal* 61:4 (March 1962), pp. 259-267; "Part 3—Aspects of the Effect of Light on Deterioration," *Museums Journal* 62:1 (June 1962), pp. 337-346; "Part 4—Viewing the Object," *Museums Journal* 62:3 (December 1962), pp. 178-186.

Harris, J.B. "Museum Lighting," *Museums Journal* 63:1 & 2 (June-September 1963), pp. 36-42.

Hatt, Robert T. "Seven Lighting Problems: Seven Solutions," *Curator* III:4 (1960), pp. 361-370.

Howard, Richard F. "Museum Lighting," *Museum News* 40:7 (March 1962), pp. 22-27.

Kelly, Richard. "Museum Lighting, Part III," *Museum News* 37:3 (May 1959), pp. 16-19.

"Lighting of Art Galleries and Museums," The Illuminating Engineering Society, *IES Technical Report No. 14*, London, 1970.

Lusk, Carroll, B. "Museum Lighting," *Museum News* 48:11 (November 1970); "Museum Lighting II," *Museum News* 48:12 (December 1970).

McCandless, Stanley. "Museum Lighting, Part I," *Museum News* 37:1 (March 1959), pp. 8-11; "Museum Lighting, Part II," *Museum News* 37:2 (April 1959), pp. 8-11.

U.S. National Bureau of Standards. *Protective Display Lighting of Historical Documents, A Report to the Library of Congress.* Washington, D.C.: Government Printing Office, 1953.

Care and Handling of Objects

Clapp, Ann. *Curatorial Care of Works of Art of Paper.* Oberlin, Ohio: Intermuseum Conservation Laboratory, 1974.

Dollof, Francis W., and Roy L. Perkinson. *How to Care for Works of Art on Paper.* Boston: Museum of Fine Arts, 1971.

Fall, Frieda Kay. *Art Objects, Their Care and Preservation: A Handbook for Museums and Collectors.* LaJolla, Cal.: Laurence McGilvery, 1973.

Photographic Conservation Bibliography. Rochester, N.Y.: Graphic Arts Research Center, Rochester Institute of Technology, 1979.

Sugden, Robert P. *Care and Handling of Art Objects.* New York: Metropolitan Museum of Art, 1946.

Packing and Shipping of Valuable Objects

Bauhof, W.A. "The Package Engineer in the Museum," *Museum News* 44:4 (December 1965) pp. 27-28.

Dudley, Dorothy H. and Irma Bezold Wilkinson, and others. *Museum Registration Methods.* 3rd Ed. Rev. Washington, D.C.: American Association of Museums, 1979.

Fall, Frieda Kay. "New Industrial Packing Materials: Their Possible Uses for Museums," *Museum News* 44:4 (December 1965) Technical Supplement No. 10.

Keck, Caroline. *Safeguarding Your Collection in Travel.* Nashville, Tennessee: American Association for State and Local History, 1970.

Little, David B. "Safeguarding Works of Art: Transportation, Records and Insurance." Technical Leaflet No. 9 from *History News*, May 1963.

Stolow, Nathan. *Conservation Standards for Works of Art in Transit and on Exhibition.* Paris: UNESCO, 1979.

Sugden, Robert P. *Safeguarding Works of Art: Storage, Packing, Transportation and Insurance.* New York: Metropolitan Museum of Art, 1948.

Security

Alsford, Denis B. *An Approach to Museum Security.* Ottawa: Canadian Museums Association, 1975.

Darling, Don D. "Guidelines for a Security Consultant," *Security World*, April 1976, 13:34, 63.

Keck, Caroline K., et al. *A Primer on Museum Security.* Cooperstown: New York State Historical Association, 1966.

Lewis, Ralph H. *Manual for Museums.* Washington, D.C.: National Park Service, 1976.

Mason, Donald L. *The Fine Art of Art Security.* New York: Von Nostrand Reinhold Co., 1979.

Security World, published by Security World Publishing Company, 2639 South La Cienaga Boulevard Los Angeles, California 90034.

Shirar, Gerald. *Protecting Works of Art.* Washington, D.C.: American Society for Industrial Security, 1978.

Tillotson, Robert G. *Museum Security.* Paris: International Council of Museums, 1977.

Environment, Conservation and Energy

Books and Articles

Feller, R.L. "Control of Deteriorating Effects of Light Upon Museum Objects," *Museum* (ICOM), Vol. XVII, No. 2, 1964.

Harrison, Lawrence S. *Report on the Deteriorating Effects of Modern Light Sources.* New York: Metropolitan Museum of Art, 1953.

Leene, Jentina E. *Textile Conservation.* Washington, D.C.: Smithsonian Institution, 1972.

Matthai, Robert A. "Energy Conservation & Management: A Critical Challenge for Cultural Institutions." *Technology & Conservation*, Spring 1978.*

Matthai, Robert A. ed. *Energy Conservation and Historic Preservation: A Resource Booklet.* Washington, D.C.: American Association of Museums Energy Committee, September 1978.*

———. *Protection of Cultural Properties During Energy Emergencies.* Washington, D.C.: American Association of Museums, March 1978.*

Plenderleith, H.J. *The Conservation of Antiquities and Works of Art.* London: Oxford University Press, 1956.

*Obtained free from the Energy Information Clearing House, Box 241, New York, N.Y. 10024 or from The American Association of Museums, 1055 Thomas Jefferson Street, N.W., Washington, D.C. 20007

Stolow, Nathan. "Notes on the Measurement of Relative Humidity and Temperature for Museums." *AAM Energy Workshop Series*, September 26, 1977.*

Weiss, Susan E. "Proper Exhibition Lighting: Protecting Collections from Damage," *Technology & Conservation*, Spring 1977.

Periodicals

Technology & Conservation (of Art, Architecture and Antiquities), published by The Technology Organization Inc., 1 Emerson Place, Boston, MA 02114 (sent free to qualified persons in the arts, architecture and antiquities)

Studies in Conservation, published by the International Institute for Conservation of Historic and Artistic Works, 608 Grand Building, Trafalgar Square, London WC 2N5HN, England

Exhibit Evaluation

Borhegyi, Stephan F. "Museum Exhibits, How to Plan and Evaluate Them," *Midwest Museums Quarterly* 32:2 (Spring 1963).

Screven, C. G. "A Bibliography on Visitor Education Research," *Museum News*, 1979, Vol. 57, No. 4.

Shettel, H.H. "An Evaluation of Existing Criteria for Judging the Quality of Science Exhibits," *Curator*, Vol. XI, No. 2, (American Museum of Natural History) New York, 1968.

Shettel, H.H.; Butcher, M; Cotton, T.S.; Northrup, J.; and D.C. Slough. "Strategies for Determining Exhibit Effectiveness." American Institutes for Research (AIR-E95-4168-FR) April 1968.

Wolf, Robert L., Barbara Timitz, Mary Andis, and Carey Tisdal. *New Perspectives on Evaluating Museums and Museum Programs: An Annotative Bibliography.* Washington, D.C.: Office of Museum Programs, Smithsonian Institution, 1978.

The Handicapped *(also see Sources for the Handicapped)*

Beechel, Jacques. "Interpretation for Handicapped Persons," *Journal of Environmental Education*, Vol. 6, No. 4, 1975.

Callow, Kathy. "Museums and the Disabled." *Museums Journal*, September 1974.

Heakes, Norma. "Serving the Handicapped," *Royal Ontario Museum Journal*, Vol. 1, Spring 1966.

Kenney, Alice P. *Access to the Past: Museum Programs and Handicapped Visitors.* Nashville: American Association for State and Local History, 1980.

Moore, George. "Displays for the Sightless." *Museums Journal*, March 1969.

Stevens, Alicia. "Seeing By Touch in a Museum," *Rehabilitation Teacher*, Vol. 4, No. 12, (December 1972).

Switzer, Mary. "The Enjoyment of the Arts: Another Aspect of Rehabilitation," *Workers for the Blind*, Washington, D.C., 1967.

Chapter 14

Index